# Body – The Greatest Gadget

## *"A human is not a being; he is a becoming. He is an ongoing process, nothing is fixed."*

Over 15,000 years ago, in the upper regions of the Himalayas, a yogi appeared. Nobody knew where he came from or what his origins were. He just came and sat absolutely still. They did not know his name so they called him the first yogi. "*Adi*" means "first," so they called him "Adiyogi." People gathered in huge numbers because his presence was quite extraordinary. They waited, hoping a miracle would happen, but he just sat unmoving for months on end, completely oblivious to everyone around. They could not even tell whether he was breathing or not; the only sign of life was tears of ecstasy dribbling out of his eyes. If someone just sits without saying a word, for the first ten minutes you would wait for something to happen. If he still does not say anything, within thirty minutes people will slowly start leaving. If he says nothing for two hours, half the people would have vanished. After six hours, maybe just three or four people would remain. This is exactly what happened to Adiyogi. People gathered in large numbers because they were waiting for a miracle to happen. Their idea of a miracle was firecrackers – some sound and light – which did not happen. They did not have the intelligence to see that a miracle had already happened: if someone simply sits for months on end, that means he is no longer ruled by the physical.

The nature of your physical existence is various levels of compulsiveness. Every few hours, you want to eat and drink. If you eat and drink, you will want to go to the bathroom. If you do that, again you will want to eat. If you eat, you will want to

*Body: The Greatest Gadget*

# Contents

# Contents

# Introduction

"Body" means different things to different people. For a child, the body and its functions are unfamiliar and new. He is coming to grips with the body's basic processes and is learning to maintain and preserve it. For a youth, the body is a vehicle fuelled by hormones, and all it takes to hijack one's attention is a handsome face or a svelte body. For someone approaching middle age, the body begins to reveal its true quality – transient and temporary. Limbs, organs, and sinews, once unworthy of notice, now begin to nag and demand consideration. For the old, body means pain and difficulty. Good health, long taken for granted, falls prey to aches and ailments, and one begins to wonder – "Is there really no more to life than this?"

Unfortunately, most people experience their body as just flesh and bone. It is seen as a source of either pain or physical pleasure, and its most subtle and profound aspects are never discovered. The medical physiology and biological functions of the body are only the outer shell. In the yogic sciences, the body is revered and recognized as an intricately crafted system which is constantly connected to and pulsating with every atom in the existence. For a yogi, the body is the supreme instrument, a tool to access and experience the entire cosmos. Through various yogic practices, one can delve layer by layer into the very roots of the body, refining the human system to such a point that it can become the very axis of the Universe. It is Sadhguru's life and work to bring these ancient technologies, designed to explore and experience the immensity of human potential, into the life of modern man.

The collection of discourses found in this book explores the yogic physiology and many subtle dimensions of the body. Sadhguru explains how yoga can reveal the very source of an ailment, and looks at ways to restructure the body so that it can be completely free of disease. He also introduces its basic building blocks – the five elements of earth, water, air, fire, and space. Speaking about the all-encompassing nature of these elements, Sadhguru tells us that "in terms of health, wellbeing, perception, knowing, enlightenment – everything is handled if only you know how to keep these five elements properly." We learn of the potency of just one breath, and its ability to give us mastery over life and death. Sadhguru introduces us to the profound science of *yogasanas,* and explains how the practice of *hata yoga* aligns the system so that "it becomes capable of experiencing the cosmos itself."

This book is an introduction to the most sophisticated and incredible gadget on the planet. It is a first step on an intriguing and exciting journey that culminates in total mastery of the system, allowing us to stay rooted in the physical, and yet taste the beyond. Above all, the book is a glimpse of a possibility to live and function in a way that most human beings would consider superhuman.

**English Publications**
**Isha Foundation**

sleep. This is the way of the body. But Adiyogi simply sat there for months. Those who came to see him out of mere curiosity, left – they missed the miracle.

Only seven hardcore people stuck on. They pleaded with him, "Please, we want to know what you know."

He dismissed them, "This is not for people who are seeking entertainment. This takes something else. Go away."

But they hung on. Seeing their perseverance, he said, "Okay, I will give you a preparatory step. Do this for some time, after that we'll see."

These seven men prepared and prepared. Days rolled into weeks, weeks into months, and months into years; still, he ignored them.

After eighty-four years of *sadhana,*[1] on the day when the summer solstice shifted to the winter solstice – when the sun's run in relation to the earth shifted from the northern run to the southern run – Adiyogi just happened to look at them. He saw they had become truly shining human beings, perfect receptacles for transmitting his knowledge. He could not ignore them anymore. He observed them for the next twenty-eight days, from that full moon day to the next full moon day. Then, he decided to teach. Because the sun had shifted to the south, he faced south and with these seven beings, began exploring the mechanics of life, which we today call "yoga." Because he turned south, he was called, Dakshinamurti, which means, "the Southern One" or "the One who looks South." That full moon day is known as Guru Pournami, or the Guru's full moon, because the first Guru was born – Adiyogi became the Adi Guru.

This day is extremely significant because for the first time in the history of humanity, someone opened up this possibility that if you are willing to strive for it, you can consciously evolve

---

1   Spiritual practices which are used as a means to realization.

from your present state to another. Until then, people believed – "This is how God made us and that is all." For the first time, Adiyogi opened up this possibility that the framework of your present making is not your limit; you can cross this framework and move into a completely different dimension of existence.

Charles Darwin told us that we were all monkeys, then our tails fell away and we became human. You know the story. When you were a monkey, you did not choose to be a human being – nature just pushed you on. But once you become human, unconscious evolution is finished for you. You can only evolve consciously. Once you have become human, certain choices and possibilities have opened up for you; a freedom has come into your life.

"Human" is not an established state, rather, it is a state of flux. This moment you can be godlike, the next moment you can be a brute. You may have seen with yourself – you are wonderful this moment, nasty the next moment, beautiful the next moment, and ugly the next. What you call as "myself" is not an established state. It can be anything any moment of the day. A human is not a *being;* he is a *becoming.* He is an ongoing process – a possibility. For this possibility to be made use of, there is a whole system of understanding the mechanics of how this life functions and what we can do with it, which we refer to as yoga.

Unfortunately, if you utter the word "yoga," people think it is about sitting in some impossible posture. Postures are just a miniscule aspect of yoga. Yoga is not just about twisting your body, standing on your head or holding your breath – a circus artist can do all these things better than most yogis. Yoga means, in your experience, everything has become one.

The word "yoga" means union. What is the union? What can unite with what? Right now, your idea of who you are – your sense and experience of who you are – is very strong. You are here as an individual, but what the trees exhale, you inhale, and what you exhale, they inhale. Or in other words, one half of your lung is hanging up there. Without it, your lungs within would be dysfunctional. Yet, in your experience, you think this individual is everything.

This is not everything. Not only in terms of breath – every subatomic particle in your body is in constant transaction with everything else in the existence according to modern physics. If this transaction stops, you will cease to exist. Scientists are proving to you that the whole existence is just one energy. For a long time, the religions of the world have been saying that God is everywhere. Whether you say "God is everywhere" or you say "everything is one energy," it is still the same reality. It is just that a scientist has never experienced it, rather he has arrived at it through mathematical deductions. A religious person has not experienced it either; he believes it because it has been written in some scripture or declared by someone. If you are a hard case, who is not willing to settle for deductions or belief systems, you want to know it for yourself. Then you become a yogi.

If you want to know for yourself, you must turn inward. Today, people are making serious efforts to know themselves by reading books. I am not against books. If you are reading a book to know about a nation or business or to learn engineering, it is fine. But reading a book to know about yourself is silly. You are here, alive and kicking! It is alright if you are reading a book to get inspired to take a step inward, but if you want to know something, you must look inward. You cannot read a book and know about yourself. After you are dead, if you have lived an interesting life, somebody may read about you, but when you are alive, you should not read about yourself. That is not the way to know yourself. In fact, the more learned you become, the more you realize that you actually know nothing. Only a fool who read half a book thinks he knows everything. Even if you read all the libraries of the world, you will still not know anything.

But if you turn inward for just one moment, everything that is worth knowing in the existence can be known.

There are very beautiful stories in our tradition, in terms of perception and experiencing life. You have heard of the Rig Veda? This is the most ancient book on the planet. It was not written down; it was transmitted verbally from generation to generation. The Rig Veda describes certain constellations and arrangements of galaxies in great detail, with proper diagrams and mathematical calculations. These constellations are not visible to the naked eye. Today, scientists are able to view them with very powerful telescopes, but how did they see them thousands of years ago? They saw, but not with their eyes, because everything that can be perceived in the existence can be grasped in a single moment if you just turn inward. The whole cosmos is here.

*"It is uncanny that today's neuroscientists are saying there is no way a human being can get any more brainy than the way he is right now."*

The body is a pot that has been churned out of the solar potter's wheel. How the solar system spins determines how the body will be and everything that happens to the solar system also happens to the body. Adiyogi said, "Your body has evolved to a point where further evolution is not possible unless something fundamental changes about the solar system."

It is uncanny that today's neuroscientists are saying that the human brain cannot evolve any further. There is no way a human being can get any brainier than the way he is right now. He can only get to use his brain better, he cannot grow it further because the only way to do that would be to either increase the size of the neurons, or increase the number of neurons in the brain. If you increase the size of the neurons, the amount of wiring that would go into it would not be sustainable because it would consume too much energy. If you increase the number of neurons, communication between them will not be coherent. The only way a human being can get more intelligent is by creating more coherence. If that is achieved, one will seem to be more intelligent, but actually it is only better utilization. No enhancement of brain has really happened because physical laws will not permit us to go further than this.

But physiological transformation or evolution is not the only evolution that is happening. Purely physiological evolution is only the first phase. After physical evolution happens, the evolutionary process shifts from physical to other dimensions. From animal to human being, evolution has happened on different dimensions. Above all, the fundamental consciousness has evolved.

The whole significance of spirituality is in its various methods to bring more of you into a conscious process. You may have heard of yogis performing seemingly unnatural feats – somebody stops his heart, somebody stops something else. These are people who learned yoga, but had a desire to become circus artists. But fundamentally, the significance of this is that even an involuntary part of your system can be made into a conscious process, where you decide the pace at which your heart should go. It is not an involuntary process any more.

# Body – An Instrument

Recently, some cell phone companies in India took a survey and found that ninety-seven percent of people are using only seven percent of the capabilities that are there in an ordinary phone. I am not talking about the smart phone, I am talking about the "dumb" phones. If they remove ninety percent of the electronics, most people will not know the difference, and they can even give a five-hundred-rupee discount. The customers will be happy, the companies will be happy!

In that little gadget, you are using only seven percent. So what about your system? This is *the* gadget. Every damn gadget has come out of this. What percentage of this gadget do you think you are employing? It is well below one percent, because for your survival process, to conduct your life in the material world, you do not even need one percent of your system's potential. Your body is capable of perceiving the whole cosmos. If you prepare it properly, it is like an antenna – if you hold it in the right position, it can grasp everything in the existence.

When it comes to physical prowess, you cannot compete with a single animal. Even if you take an insect, for the tiny piece of life that it is, just look at its physical prowess. It can jump almost fifty to a hundred times the length of its body. If you are five or six feet tall, you should be jumping five hundred feet. In terms of physical prowess, any animal in nature – whether a worm, insect, bird or animal – is made far more capable than you. The human body has come with a different capability altogether.

As a human being, you have a few different possibilities – a certain capability that you can do something beyond your instinct of survival. That is most important. Yet, most human beings instead of looking beyond the needs of survival, have just

*Body: The Greatest Gadget*

raised their standards of survival. Survival at one time meant getting a meal or two a day. Now, survival means you must have a Mercedes. We are raising the bar, but it is still only survival. This is an unintelligent way of using the human mechanism which has come with a different possibility altogether. This body can be just a mass of flesh, driven by simple instincts within you, or it can be made into a tremendous instrument – an instrument which can bring the Divine into your direct experience.

## *"The very life process is a great miracle. The very way you have become all this, from being two little cells, is it not a miracle?"*

One fundamental aspect of yoga is learning to use your body like an instrument. Most people are so identified with their bodies that they experience it as themselves.

This human system is not a simple mechanism. You can play on it and do the kind of things that you would never have imagined possible. In your experience, when you are identified with your body and look at it as "myself," either you are proud of it or ashamed of it. Once you have such problems, you cannot use this as an instrument. There is a way to live where you can make this body an instrument that becomes the very axis of the universe.

In yoga, we refer to the human spine as the *Merudanda,* which means the axis of the Universe. "How can my spine be the axis of the Universe?" If your experience of life is limited, you will only perceive whatever is within the boundaries of your sensation as "you." If you touch an inanimate object, do you experience it as a part of yourself? The water in your cup, is it you? What if you drink it? Does it become you? Anything that you include into the boundaries of your sensation becomes you.

Today, it is a medical fact that the boundaries of your sensation, or your sensory body, has a presence beyond the physical body. Doctors are clearly saying that when a man's limb is amputated, even if the physical leg is gone, the sensory leg is still intact. He

*Body: The Greatest Gadget*

will feel pain or sensation in his limb, even though it is gone, because the sensory body has a separate experience of its own.

If you make yourself very exuberant with joy, love, or ecstasy for example, the sensory body becomes very large. If you make yourself depressed and sad, even if somebody physically touches you, you may not even notice it, because your sensory body has shrunk below the size of the physical body.

There are methods to crank up the voltage in your system and expand your sensory body. Suppose you expanded your sensory body, you could experience everything as a part of yourself. As you experience the five fingers on your hand, you can experience anything you are willing to include, as a part of yourself. If even for a moment, you experience everyone around you as a part of yourself, after that do I have to teach you morality – "Be good to this person, don't harm this person, don't kill this person?" Anything that you know as "myself," with that you are in harmony, with that there is no conflict, there is no problem. It is the other which is the problem.

You can expand your sensory body to everything; you can include the whole universe as a part of yourself. That is what we are referring to as yoga. Yoga means union. That means, the individual and the universal have become one. In your experience, only you are. Everything is you. The moment you know this experientially, not as an idea or a philosophy but in reality, when you have experienced everything as yourself, nobody needs to tell you how to be. You just know. Everything has become one within you because your sensory body has expanded in a limitless way.

If your sensory body extends to the whole universe, even then the center of this sensory body will be your spine – your experiential dimension is rooted in your spine. How the energies in your spine are functioning right now determines just about everything about your life. That is why yoga attaches enormous importance to the human spine. Medical science unfortunately has not given it that kind of significance.

The evolution of animals from invertebrates to vertebrates – from being spineless to having a spine – was a huge leap forward, in terms of development of the body. After that, moving from a horizontal spine to a vertical spine was an even bigger step in the development of the brain.

There is enough scientific understanding to show that the development of the brain began only after the spine became erect. It is from this understanding that certain yogis never lie down. Even if they have to sleep, they sleep sitting up, because when someone is trying to evolve in a great way within this lifespan, remaining in vertical postures as much as possible is very essential. If you know how to be sufficiently relaxed in your erect postures, you will see that the need to lie down and the need to sleep will come down quite dramatically. Only because you are tense in your vertical posture, the need for sleep goes on increasing.

A yogi is somebody who is transforming his body and making it like a ladder to heaven. For that, having a little bit of mastery over the spine becomes essential. That is why in tradition, it is said that there are thirty-three steps to heaven. Some people started drawing artwork depicting heaven with God sitting at the top of thirty-three steps. That is not the point. There are thirty-three bones in your spine. This can be a painful spine, or this can be made into a ladder you climb upon and reach the highest level of consciousness, pleasure, and blissfulness within yourself.

One aspect of yoga is to make all possibilities, even the spiritual possibilities of life, almost like a physical science. You don't have to start with a single belief. You just start with simple understanding and start experimenting with it. For example, if you take any chemical reaction, let us say you put two parts of hydrogen and one part of oxygen together, you will get water. Whoever does it, whether a great scientist or a fool does it, the same thing will happen. Similarly, in yoga, we made it very simple – you do this, this and this, things will happen.

For the sake of understanding and experiencing, we made all aspects of a human being into five bodies, so that you can understand it as a physical entity. These five layers are: *annamaya kosha, manomaya kosha, pranamaya kosha, vignanamaya kosha, and anandamaya kosha.*

The first layer, *annamaya kosha,* means the "food body." We are calling it food body because what you call as "my body" right now is just a heap of food that you have accumulated. When you were born, your body was so small, and now it has become so big, just because of the food you have eaten.

The second layer is called *manomaya kosha* or the "mental body." Doctors nowadays, say that you are psychosoma – a mind-body combination. People who have psychosomatic diseases, for example, become physically ill because of a certain state of mind.

Like there is a physical body, there is something called the mental body. Every cell in the body has its own intelligence, so there is a whole mental body. Whatever happens on the level of the mind naturally happens on the level of the physiology and whatever happens on the level of the physiology in turn happens on the level of the mind.

Your body, mind, and emotions are the only things that are in your experience right now. You can infer that if these three things have to happen the way they are happening, there must be an energy that makes them happen. Without energy, all this cannot be happening. For example, a microphone amplifies sound. Even if you do not know anything about the microphone, you can infer that there is a source that powers it. The third dimension of your body is referred to as the energy body or the *pranamaya kosha.*

The energy body reverberates in a certain way, and whichever way it reverberates, that is the way your mental body and physical body happen. The basic work of yoga is mostly on the level of *pranamaya kosha* because if you handle this properly, physical wellness is naturally taken care of.

*Pranamaya kosha* is the fundamental energy in all physical creation. If you have mastery over your *prana,* or energy, it is not only about your life and health, you also have mastery over the situations around you. As your energies become more balanced, suddenly your life situations work out the way you want even before you think about it. You do not have to slog with life anymore. Whatever you do, there is no pressure on you because everything just falls into place. If you work twenty-four hours a day, day after day, still there is no such thing as stress or pressure on you.

If you feel my pulse, most of the time it is below forty, if I am hungry. After I have eaten, it is somewhere around forty-two to forty-five. If I am physically active, it may raise to fifty, fifty-four. Only if I run up a staircase or something, it will raise higher than that. When the body is like this, it is as if you are in deep slumber all the time, fast asleep, but wide awake. Once you are like this, there is no such thing as stress.

If these three dimensions, the physical body, the mental body, and the energy body, are kept in a certain state of alignment, what is deeper than that begins to function by its own nature. That dimension is the very source of creation.

People see miraculous changes in their physiological and psychological conditions simply because once your energy body is in proper balance and full flow, disease cannot exist in you physiologically or psychologically. It does not matter what it is. This is like your car was not starting, so you pushed it, kicked it, cursed it – you did everything. Your mechanic came and simply touched it, and suddenly everything is okay. Similarly, with your body, you do not understand what is where and how it is functioning. Whatever you do, it does not work. Then, with just a simple process – everything seems to be okay. There are thousands upon thousands of people who have dropped their ailments by doing simple yogic practices and balancing their system. For a thinking mind, this looks like a miracle.

Anything that you do not understand, you tend to call it a miracle. Let us say you don't know anything about electricity, and I tell you, "If I touch the wall, the whole hall will be flooded in light." Will you believe me? If I press the switch and the whole place becomes light, you will think I am the messenger of God, or the son of God, or God himself, just because you do not understand how it functions. Anything that you do not understand becomes a miracle in your mind. The very life process is a great miracle. The very way you have become all this from being two little cells, is it not a miracle? Everything about life is miraculous. Otherwise, if you start explaining it, nothing is a miracle.

These three dimensions, the physical body, the mental body, and the energy body are physical in nature. They are getting subtler as you go – from grossly physical to a little subtler, to much more subtle, but they are all physical in nature. You can clearly see that the light bulb is physical, but the electricity which makes it glow is also physical, the light that it throws out is also physical. Similarly, these three layers are of physical nature.

*Vignananaya kosha* is of a completely different nature. There is no appropriate word in English so it is generally referred to as "etheric body" or spiritual body. This is a transitory body. Transitory in the sense, it is moving from physical nature into non-physical nature. The intermediate space or the intermediate state is referred to as "ether" or *"vignana."*

This is the dimension where if transformation happens, it is truly forever. Suppose we teach your body to do yoga. If you do *asanas* for six months you will feel so much better physically, mentally, and in every way. But if you do not do it for another six months, you will once again come back to your old states. Whatever you do on the level of the physical body can be easily reversed. If you reorient your mind to look at life in a different way, you feel like you are reborn. But very easily you can revert to your old ways. Whatever you do on the physiological and psychological level can easily be reversed if the person is not willing to go that way. Suppose with *pranayam* or *kriyas* you alter the pranic energy, the change lasts much longer, but after some time that will also revert.

If you make the necessary transformation in the etheric body, it is forever. It is for life and beyond – nothing changes. The difference between a Guru and a teacher is just this, a teacher will teach you methods with which you can change your *annamaya kosha, manomaya kosha* and *pranamaya kosha,* but he cannot touch your *vignanamaya kosha.* A Guru works on your *vignanamaya kosha.* Once he touches that, everything is changed dramatically because this change is permanent. It is beyond the physical dimension, and it is always permanent.

The fifth layer is called *anandamaya kosha* which means "bliss body." Does it mean there is a bubble of bliss sitting inside of you? No, this is a dimension beyond the physical. Anything that is non-physical can neither be defined nor described by us, so we can only talk about it in terms of our experience. We only know that when we touch it, we become blissful, so from our experience, we say this is bliss body. It does not mean its nature is bliss; it is just that it makes us blissful.

For example, if you are talking about sugar, you say it is sweet. Sweet is not the nature of the sugar. That is the experience that it creates within you. When you put it in your mouth you taste it as sweet, so you call it sweet. Just like that, bliss is not the nature of the innermost core. It is non-physical, we cannot define or describe that which is non-physical, so we are speaking in child's language. If there is a speaker system here, if a child comes and touches it, he does not know what it is, so he says, *"Boom, boom, boom"* – I think in America they call it a boom box. That is child's language. Similarly, calling it bliss body is child's language. We are speaking about it in terms of our experience, not in terms of its nature.

If the three physical dimensions of the body are not aligned, you never get to touch this core. Yoga is about aligning these three, so that the innermost core becomes available to you. Once you touch it, you are blissful by your own nature. To be blissful becomes absolutely natural. Every moment of your life, one can be ecstatic and blissful. Above all, only when you touch the non-physical dimension of life, we say you are spiritual. If these three are properly aligned, your journey through life becomes absolutely effortless and to the fullest potential possible without any stress or strain. You can pass through this life without the life process leaving a single scratch upon you. You can play with life whichever way you want, but life cannot leave a single scratch upon you. Every human being is capable of living like this.

When it comes to external realities, each one of us is differently capable, but when it comes to inner realities, all of us are equally capable. It has not happened to people because people have never applied themselves in that direction. People have never paid attention to the inner. They always believed that if we fix the outside, everything will be okay. But the affluent classes in the world are sufficient proof that fixing the outside is not enough for life. You need to do something about yourself too. Once your interiority is fixed, then whatever the kind of external situations, you can still live a full life. If your interiority is not managed, it does not matter what we have achieved on the outside, everything goes waste. With great effort, people reach success, only to suffer success. How much effort it has taken! But when they get there, they cannot enjoy it, they only suffer it because the internal has not been taken care of at all.

It takes a certain amount of awareness for a human being to realize that the essence of his life, the quality of his life is not decided by what is outside, but by what is within him. This has been completely misinterpreted. People concluded that if you want to be spiritual, you must give up everything outside. It is not about giving up or not giving up. Whether you are spiritual or otherwise, you anyway breathe, eat food and drink water. Whether you eat good food or bad food is the only choice you have. So it is not about giving up. It is a shift of focus where you see that if you do not handle the internal appropriately, the quality of your life cannot be good.

The quality of your life is decided not by what kind of clothes you wear, what kind of car you drive or what kind of home you live in, but by how peaceful and joyful you are within yourself. This is essentially the quality of your life. Everything else is done to get there. If this does not happen, everything else goes waste.

*Body: The Greatest Gadget*

## *"Certain qualities in nature have been identified as masculine, while other qualities have been identified as feminine."*

**Questioner: You have talked about the spine determining the nature of our experience. Can you tell us a little bit more about that?**

**Sadhguru:** Within the spine, if you know its physical construction, you will know there are two holes on either side of the spine which are like conduit pipes for all the nerves to pass. These are the *Ida* and the *Pingala,* the left and the right channels.

In the *pranamaya kosha* or the energy body, there are 72,000 *nadis. Nadis* are pathways or channels in the system. If you cut this body and see, you will not see them. But as you become more aware of the movement of energy, you will see energy is not moving at random, it is moving in particular patterns. There are 72,000 different ways in which the energy moves. These 72,000 *nadis* spring from three basic *nadis* – *Ida, Pingala,* and *Sushumna.*

*Ida* and *Pingala* represent the two dimensions of life which we symbolize as feminine and masculine. This is not in terms of gender or about being male or female, but in terms of certain qualities in nature. Certain qualities in nature have been identified as masculine, while other qualities have been identified as feminine. You may be a man, but if your *Ida* is more pronounced, the feminine may be dominant in you. You may be a woman, but if your *Pingala* is more pronounced, the masculine may be dominant in you. It has nothing to do with you being a man or a woman. When we say masculine and feminine, on the level of your mind, *Pingala* represents the logical dimension of the mind; *Ida* represents the intuitive dimension of the mind.

Another way of looking at this is to symbolize these two aspects as sun and moon. *Pingala* is represented by the sun and *Ida* is represented by the moon, because one is outgoing and aggressive, the other is reflective and receptive. The outgoing nature is considered masculine. The reflective and receptive nature is considered feminine. These are two halves of life. Without one, the other cannot happen. All energy also functions this way. Electricity cannot function without positive and negative. Nobody can say which is more important than the other because one cannot exist without the other. These two aspects of life are represented by these two channels of *Ida* and *Pingala*.

In Indian culture, two traditions evolved, which identified with the sun and with the moon. Some were referred to as the *Suryavamshis*[2] and the others were referred to as the *Chandravamshis*.[3] A whole system of spiritual process, social process, political process, and economic process evolved based on these two dimensions. Even today it is manifest, but one may not recognize it.

These are two different dimensions of function on the planet. Some people are operating out of the moon within them, some people are operating with the sun within them, but both are problematic. A few people are operating using both of them evenly; they are the solution for this planet.

You will constantly see, very "good" people will go about creating enormous problems. If two very nice people get married – how much trouble they create! The reason is just this, they are operating from two different dimensions and trying to meet – it will not happen. It will only work as a hit and run, it will

---

2   Those belonging to the Solar Dynasty.
3   Those belonging to the Lunar Dynasty.

*Body: The Greatest Gadget*

not work as a combination. Only endless quarrel and friction will happen. Any number of people sit down and try to analyze, "What is the problem? We don't have any problem, both of us are great, why is there a problem?" There is no logical reason, but still there is a problem.

Husband and wife are a classic example, but it is not just happening between husband and wife. It is happening everywhere, between everybody, in different scales and modes. Only those people who manage these two things equally, who find expression to both the sun and moon within them in an equal manner, will be the ones coming out with solutions. All the others keep coming out with problems. There is nothing wrong with them, they are very nice people, but they are problematic. Don't think two bad people are fighting on the planet. It is always two good people who are fighting on the planet. The more good they think they are, the more they quarrel, isn't it?

Most people live and die in *Ida* and *Pingala*. *Sushumna,* the central space, is the most significant aspect of human physiology. Life really begins only when energies enter into *Sushumna,* but for the majority, it remains dormant.

Fundamentally, *Sushumna* is attribute-less, it has no quality of its own. It is like empty space. If there is empty space, you can create anything you want. Once energies enter into *Sushumna,* we say you attain to *Vairagya. "Raga"* means color. *"Vairagya"* means no color, you have become transparent. If you have become transparent, if what is behind you is red, you turn red too. If what is behind you is blue, you turn blue. You are unprejudiced. Wherever you are, you become a part of that, but nothing sticks to you. If you are among red people, you can be totally red because you are transparent, but the redness does not stick to you for a moment.

Only if you are in a state of *Vairagya,* will you dare to explore all dimensions of life. If any color sticks to you, if red has stuck to you, you will resist going into the green. If green has stuck to you, you will resist going into the blue. If anything sticks to you, you will resist the next one, because you developed a prejudice of "this is right, that is wrong, this is okay, that is not okay." It restricts the flow of life.

Above all, once the energies enter into *Sushumna,* you attain to a new kind of balance. Right now, you may be reasonably balanced, but if for some reason the outside situation goes crazy, you will also go crazy in reaction to that because the nature of *Ida* and *Pingala* is reactive. But once the energies enter *Sushumna,* you earn an inner balance. There is a certain space within you which never gets disturbed, which is never in any kind of turmoil; a space which cannot be touched by outside situations. Only if you create this stable situation within yourself, will you dare to scale the peaks of consciousness. If we want to explore other dimensions of life within ourselves, it is very important that we create a certain stability that the fear of suffering is taken away. Only when you create that, you will dare to explore different dimensions of life.

# "Very few people are mad enough to live their life with total abandon."

**Questioner: Sadhguru, will you please enlighten us on the chakras in our body?**

**Sadhguru:** Chakras – there is too much chakra talk going on everywhere. Especially in the West, wherever you go, there are "wheel alignment centers" where they "align" your chakras and this and that. From yoga studios to chiropractic doctors, everybody is "doing" chakras these days. It has become a fashion.

What is a chakra? There are 114 chakras in the body. There are actually many more, these are the major ones. You can see them as 114 junction boxes or confluence of *nadis*. These junctions are always in the form of triangles. Chakra literally means a wheel or a circle because it symbolizes movement from one dimension to another. It is referred to as a chakra, but it is actually a triangle.

Among these 114, two are outside the body and 112 are within the body. Among these 112, there are seven major chakras. For most people, three of these are active, the remaining are either dormant or mildly active. You do not have to activate all the 114 chakras to live a physical life. You can live quite a complete life and go with just a few of them. If you activate all the 114, you will have no sense of body; you will have no feeling of body at all. This is the essence of yoga – to activate your energy system in such a way that your sense of body is constantly being lowered. If you sit here, you are in the body, but you are no longer the body.

In South India, there was a yogi by the name of Sadashiva Brahmendra. He was a *nirkaya,* which literally means a "bodiless yogi." He had no sense of body. When one has no sense of body, wearing clothes does not even occur to such a person. He just walked naked. And when one has no sense of body, he has no sense of boundary and property. One day, on the banks of river Cauvery, he happened to walk into the king's garden. The king was sitting there relaxing with his queens. Sadashiva Brahmendra walked into the garden naked, in front of these women – he had no sense of who is a man and who is a woman. The king got angry, "Who is this fool who is walking naked in front of my women?" He sent his soldiers and ordered them, "Find out who this fool is." The soldiers ran behind him and called the yogi. He did not turn back, he simply kept walking. The soldiers got angry, took out their sword and struck him, severing his right arm. But he did not even break his stride. He kept walking.

Seeing this, the soldiers were terrified. They realized this was no ordinary man. Even if his arm is chopped, he keeps walking. The king and soldiers ran behind him, fell at his feet, and brought him back to the garden. He lived in that garden for the rest of his life and left his body there. There have been innumerable situations like this.

If I sit here for two or three days without food or sleep, I will carry on the same way. If your energy is in a certain way, you will have no sense of body; you never think of food or toilet. When you have the time, you eat, you relieve yourself. If there is no time, you can go the whole day without food, simply because your energies are in a certain hyped state that they do not constantly require anything external.

What is it that the chakras do in the system? What is their role within you? The seven fundamental chakras are known as *Muladhara, Swadhishthana, Manipuraka, Anahata, Vishuddhi, Agna, and Sahasrar.* Physiologically, *Muladhara* is located at

*Body: The Greatest Gadget*

the perineum. There is a little space between the anal outlet and the genital organ – that space is *Muladhara*. *"Mula,"* means the root or source, and *"adhar,"* means the foundation. In the engineering of the body, this is the base. If you wish to grow, you need to cultivate this.

If I speak in terms of lower and higher chakras, it can easily be misunderstood. It is like comparing the foundation of a building to the roof – the roof is not superior to the foundation. The foundation of the building is more basic to the building than the roof. The quality, life span, stability and security of the building depend, to a large extent, on the foundation rather than the roof. But in terms of language, the roof is higher, and the foundation is lower.

In the physical body, your energies need to be in the *Muladhara* chakra to some extent. Otherwise, you cannot exist. But if the *Muladhara* chakra alone becomes dominant, food and sleep will be the predominant factors in your life.

Chakras have more than one dimension to them. One dimension is their physical existence, but they also have a spiritual dimension. This means that they can be completely transformed into a new dimension. For example, if you bring the right kind of awareness, the same *Muladhara* that craves food and sleep, can become absolutely free from the process of food and sleep. If one wants to go beyond food and sleep, one needs to transform the *Muladhara* to an evolved state.

The second chakra is *Swadhishthana*. *Swadhishthana* means "the abode of the self." If your energies move into *Swadhishthana,* you seek to enjoy the physical world in so many ways. If you look at a pleasure seeker, you will see that his life and his experience of life are just a little more intense than someone who is only about food and sleep. The *Swadhishthana* chakra is located just above the genital organ.

If your energy moves into the *Manipuraka* chakra, located just below the navel, you become a doer in the world. You are all about action. You may be a businessman, or a politician or some other field where a lot of activity is needed.

*Manipuraka* is the maintenance center. It is the only point in the whole body where all the 72,000 *nadis* meet and re-distribute themselves. If you have a certain mastery over your *Manipuraka*, you can fix the time and date of your death. Generally, it is very important for a yogi to know when he will die, or otherwise, he fixes his time of death himself, because he wants to die gracefully, as he lived gracefully. It is very important for him how he dies.

If your energies move into the *Anahata*, which is just below that spot where your rib cage meets, you are a creative person. "*Anahata*" literally means the "un-struck." If you want to make any sound, you have to strike two objects together. The *un-struck* sound is called "*Anahata*." *Anahata* is like a transition between your lower chakras and higher chakras, between survival instincts and the instinct to liberate yourself.

If you look at the chakras as two different dimensions, the *Manipuraka, Swadhishthana,* and *Muladhara* are more concerned with keeping the body stable and rooted. These are the earth qualities. The more you ascribe your energies to these three centers, the more your qualities will become earthy, more in the grip of nature. The upper ones, the *Vishuddhi, Agna* and *Sahasrar,* are three centers which are always taking you away. If your energies become dominant in these centers, it will take you away from the pull of the earth. These centers make you receptive to another force which we normally refer to as Grace.

Between the first three and the last three, the first three are pulling you towards the Earth, the last three are pulling you away from the Earth. *Anahata* is a balance between the two. It

*Body: The Greatest Gadget*

is symbolized by two interlocked triangles, one pointing down, another pointing up, forming a star between them. Many religions in the world have used this symbol, because somewhere in their culture, somebody realized his original nature through *Anahata* and naturally found this interlocking triangle within himself, because that is how the *Anahata* meets.

The next chakra is the *Vishuddhi,* which is located in the pit of your throat. The word "*Vishuddhi*" literally means a "filter," because if *Vishuddhi* becomes powerful, you have the ability to filter everything that enters you. Shiva's center is supposed to be *Vishuddhi,* and he is also known as Vishakantha[4] or Neelakantha[5] because he filters all the poison at the pit of the throat. He does not allow it to enter his system. It is not necessarily poison that you may consume through food. Poisons can enter you in so many ways. A wrong thought or emotion, the wrong kind of energy or a wrong impulse can poison your life. If your *Vishuddhi* is active, it filters everything and saves you from all these influences. Or in other words, once *Vishuddhi* is very active, that person is so powerful within himself that external nature has no influence on him. Whatever is around him does not influence him anymore. He is established within himself.

If your energies move into the *Agna* chakra, located between your eyebrows, you are intellectually enlightened; you attain to a new balance and peace within you. The outside no longer disturbs you, but you are still experientially not liberated. Once someone has attained union on the level of *Agna,* suddenly the intellectual types look stupid in front of him. Adi Shankara – the most argumentative Indian ever, such unbeatable logic – walked all across the land, looking for arguments. People were defeated in hordes. All kinds of people came to argue with him. Whoever

---

4  Lit. One who has poison in his throat.
5  Lit. One who has a blue throat.

argued with him was bound to lose. There was nobody else with that kind of logic, because the union experienced in *Agna* gives you a completely different kind of logic.

*Sahasrar* is the seventh chakra. It is not in the body, it is just outside the body. On top of the head, there is a spot known as *Brahmarandhra* or "the opening." When a child is born, there is a tender spot where the bone does not form till the child grows to a certain age. Just above that is *Sahasrar.* For most people it is dormant, it is not active. If some *sadhana* comes into your life or because of a very intense way of living, it can become active.

If energies move into *Sahasrar,* you will become ecstatic. If there isn't sufficient *sadhana* to create the necessary physiological and psychological balance, this ecstasy can become uncontrollable. You are simply so ecstatic that you do not know how to handle any other aspect of your life. So generally, as far as people are concerned, you will seem to be mad. When a person becomes like this, in the tradition they used to call them *Avadhutas* – they do not know how to handle their life. Somebody has to feed them, clean them, and take care of them. They are just ecstatic, that's all. A very wonderful state, but most people cannot afford it for so many reasons.

Fundamentally, any spiritual path can be described as a journey from the *Muladhara* to the *Sahasrar.* This journey is an evolution from one dimension to another. To move your energies from *Muladhara* to *Agna,* there are many spiritual processes and several ways, but to move from *Agna* to *Sahasrar,* there is no path. There is no particular way. One has to either jump or fall into it.

The reason why in the spiritual traditions, so much stress was always laid on the *Guru-shishya* relationship – the master-disciple relationship – is simply because of this. Paths can be charted out and methods can be taught as to how to move your energies to *Agna.* But to stabilize themselves at *Agna* and move

*Body: The Greatest Gadget*

to *Sahasrar,* where there is no path, where there is no particular method, it simply needs trust. Without trust, one will not know how, because it is like jumping into a void. Suppose, there is a big hole in the Earth, a very deep well where you cannot see the bottom. If somebody says, "Jump," either you must be utterly crazy, or have extraordinary courage, or have absolute trust in the person who is saying this. These are the only three ways you can jump. Let us discount the courage – there are very few people with that kind of mad courage who can simply jump without bothering what happens to them. You must be crazy or you must be trustful. These are the only two ways.

Very few people are mad enough to live their life with total abandon. Even a miniscule percentage of the population is not crazy enough to simply live their life with total abandon. There is caution in everybody, there is insecurity and the need to protect themselves in everybody. So that first option goes. 99.9% of the people need trust, otherwise they cannot jump. This is the reason why so much stress is laid on this relationship, because without the trust, one will never take that jump.

# The Geometry of the Cosmos

*"The whole science of yoga is to understand the geometry of your existence, because the whole existence is a certain kind of geometry, and your body is also a certain kind of geometry."*

Creation is a certain complexity of geometry. The whole Universe is geometrically perfect. That is why it stays there, otherwise it would not. If you learn to hold your body in a certain way, if the geometry of your body is in alignment with the geometry of the rest of the creation, suddenly, you will find there is a rapport which will allow you to download the whole cosmos.

These days, since "Tata Sky" and "Dishnet" have come, this problem is probably gone for you, but before that, after every rain shower, you would have to go and adjust your TV antenna properly. You would be watching your favorite soap opera or a cricket match and suddenly the image would be gone. You would have to go up and fine tune it; otherwise it would not receive anything. Only if your antenna is in a certain way, you have reception.

This body is just like that. You are here to perceive the existence. If you hold it the right way, in the right geometry, this can receive and download the whole cosmic space. To hold it in a certain way, you must keep the body in a state of ease. Otherwise, if it is in a state of rigidity or compulsion, you cannot get into that place where it becomes a receptacle of the existence – it will block it and not allow it to happen.

*Body: The Greatest Gadget*

Within your own home and office, among your friends, do you see every one of you have different levels of perception? I want you to just observe this – don't talk about this – if you find somebody among your friends or family who has a better perception than others, you can see a visible difference in the way they conduct their body. If you feel somebody is dull, they are not getting anything, see how they conduct their body. You will understand what I mean by geometry of your existence. The way you hold your body will determine everything about you.

The whole yogic system is, in a way, about adjusting the geometry of the body so that it becomes an absolute antenna for the existence to happen within you, not outside of you. You cannot know what is happening outside of you; you only know what is happening inside of you. Only if you perceive it, you know. If you do not perceive it you do not know. So, if you want to enhance your perception, you have to refine the geometry of your body. Yoga is just that.

To learn to simply sit, do you know how much yoga you have to do? A lot of training is needed for a person just to be able to sit in the right posture to do a particular kind of act. If you so much as just move the hands and legs, it changes everything. The hands and legs are very important. Even medically, you know that the maximum nerve-endings are in the hands and legs. The medical system acknowledges that your nerves are transmitting perception.

Your perception is the most important thing. Did you perceive everything that a human being can perceive or did you go unlived? That is all the question is for me. How long you lived is not at all important; how profound your experience of life is, that is most important, isn't it? If you want to perceive everything, you must learn to arrange the geometry of your system properly. That is why we start off with *asanas*, *mudras*, and *kriyas* – to arrange the energy geometry of your system in such a way that it becomes capable of experiencing the cosmos itself.

"By consciously getting your body into a certain posture, you can also elevate your consciousness, you can change the very way you feel, think, understand, and experience life simply by sitting in a particular way."

An asana is a posture. There are innumerable postures your body can take. Among these, certain postures have been identified as *yogasanas*. "Yoga" means that which takes you on to a higher dimension or higher perception of life. So, that kind of posture which leads you to a higher possibility is called a "*yogasana*."

You may have noticed that for different mental and emotional situations that you go through, your body naturally tends to take a certain posture. If you are happy, you sit one way. When you are unhappy you sit another way. When you are peaceful you sit one way, if you are angry you sit another way. Many times, you can tell what is happening with someone by just observing the way they are sitting, have you noticed? Based on this, conversely is the science of *asanas* – by consciously getting your body into a certain posture, you can also elevate your consciousness. You can change the very way you feel, think, understand, and experience life by sitting in a particular way.

*Yogasanas* are not exercises. They are very subtle processes of manipulating your energy in a certain direction. It needs to be done with a certain level of awareness. There are various levels of doing *asanas*. You can practice *asanas* just physically, or more deeply, being aware of the breath, sensations, reverberations, being aware of the *nadis*, or with appropriate mantras. You can even do *asanas* without moving a limb. That is also possible.

The science of *asanas* is known as *hata yoga*. "Ha" means sun, "ta" means moon. The first process of yoga is to bring

*Body: The Greatest Gadget*

balance between the masculine and feminine in you. Otherwise there will be no scaling of consciousness. This is why Shiva is known as Ardhanarishvara – one half of him is a woman, another half of him is a man. He is a man and the very embodiment of manhood. At the same time, he is also woman, because without bringing this balance, without cultivating these two dimensions within us, there is no reaching towards the peak, there is no question of a human being flowering to his fullest possibility. That is why the first dimension of yoga that you practice is *hata yoga*. That means the yoga of the sun and the moon is bringing balance between the masculine and the feminine. That is the first step to take.

Among the *yogasanas,* there are eighty-four basic *asanas* through which one can elevate his consciousness. When we say eighty-four *asanas,* do not think of them as just eighty-four postures. These are eighty-four systems, eighty-four ways of attaining. Out of this, if you have mastery over even a single *yogasana,* everything that is worth knowing in the existence can be known. People who have taken up *hata yoga* as their way of life generally take up one *asana* for their life's *sadhana.* This is known as *asana siddhi. Asana siddhi* means, one is able to sit in a particular way with absolute ease. For most people, whichever way they keep their body, it is not at ease. If you sit, it is not comfortable. If you stand, it is not comfortable. If you lie down, it is not comfortable. What the hell to do with this? If you give your body to the process of yoga, slowly the body becomes at ease. If you sit like this, it is absolutely at ease. It is not trying to be some other way.

A thinking mind cannot understand how a man can spend his whole life wanting to sit in a particular way. But everything that can be perceived can be perceived, by having mastery over a single physical posture. That is what *yogasana* means.

The reason why *hata yoga* has become ugly is because people start taking it like a circus. The way *hata yoga* is happening in the West scares me, because all kinds of things are done in the name of yoga, that are not yoga.

Recently, I was playing golf with a group of young people and they asked, "What do you do?"

I just ignored the question and took my shot and kept walking. They asked somebody who was walking with me, and he said, "He teaches yoga."

Immediately, they ran up to me and said, "Can you teach us something that will give us six pack abs?"

I said, "I can give you fourteen if you are interested."

This is not about sculpting your body and showing it off. This is to make the body into a fantastic vessel, a fabulous device to receive the Divine. *Hata yoga* is a phenomenal process, but today, many physical therapists and experts are writing books on *hata yoga*, making people believe it is an exercise system. It is not an exercise system. Studio yoga is unfortunately just the physical aspect of it. Teaching only the physical aspect of yoga is like having a stillborn baby. If you want a living thing, it needs to be taught in a certain way. In a proper atmosphere, with a certain sense of humility and inclusiveness about the whole process, *hata yoga* is a very fantastic process. If I do a two-day *hata yoga* program, people will burst with tears of ecstasy simply doing *asanas,* and that is the way yoga needs to be done.

*"If you travel through the breath, deep into yourself, it will take you to that point where you are tied to the body."*

**Questioner: I want to ask a question regarding breathing. Some medical professionals say, "Breath is an involuntary action. Just breathe normally." Some of the yoga people say, "Breathe deeply, it helps you to be effective." What is the real significance of this?**

**Sadhguru:** What you are asking is essentially, how is breath connected to your wellbeing? Breath is not just the exchange of oxygen and carbon dioxide. How you breathe decides many aspects of who you are right now. Have you noticed, for different levels of thought and emotion that you go through, your breath takes on different types of patterns? If you are angry, you breathe in one way. If you are peaceful, you breathe another way. If you are very happy, you breathe another way. If you are sad, you breathe another way. Whichever way you breathe, that is the way you think. Whichever way you think, that is the way you breathe.

This breath can be used in so many ways as a tool to do other things with the body and the mind. With the Shambhavi,[6] we use a very simple process of breath, but it is not about the breath. Breath is just a tool; it is just an induction. What happens is not

<hr />

6 A simple but powerful kriya offered in the Inner Engineering program, which takes 21 minutes to practice.

about the breath. *Pranayam*[7] is the science where, by consciously breathing in a particular way, the very way you think, feel and understand and experience life can be changed.

If I ask you to watch your breath, which is the most common practice people do these days, you think you are watching the breath, but actually you are not. You are only able to notice the sensations caused by the movement of air. It is like, if someone touches your hand, you think you know the touch of the other person, but actually, you only know the sensations generated within your body; you do not know how the other person feels.

Breath is like the hand of the Divine. You don't *feel* it. This breath that you do not experience is referred to as *Koorma Nadi*. I am not referring to the sensations caused by the air, I am referring to the breath itself. *Koorma Nadi* is referred to as a string which ties you with this body – an unbroken string that goes on and on. If I take away your breath, you and your body will fall apart because the being and the body are bound by the *Koorma Nadi*. This is a big deception. There are two, but they are pretending to be one. It is like marriage – they are two, but when they come out they pretend to be one. There are two people here, the body and being, two diametrically opposite ones, but they pretend that they are one.

If you travel through the breath, deep into yourself, to the deepest core of the breath, it will take you to that point where you are actually tied to the body. Once you know where you are tied and how you are tied, you can untie it at will. Consciously, you can shed the body as effortlessly as you would shed your clothes.

When you know where your clothes are tied, it is easy to drop them. When you don't know where it is tied, whichever way you pull, it does not come off. The same applies to the body.

---

7 A powerful yogic practice which uses breathing techniques to generate and direct the flow of prana (vital life energy) in the body.

*Body: The Greatest Gadget*

If you do not know how your clothes are tied, if you want to take them off, you have to tear them apart. Similarly, if you do not know where your body is tied to you, if you want to drop it, you have to damage or break it in some way. But if you know where it is tied, you can very clearly hold it at a distance. When you want to drop it, you can just drop it consciously. Life becomes very different.

When somebody willfully sheds the body completely, we say this is *Mahasamadhi*. This is what is generally referred to as *mukti,* or Ultimate liberation. You have arrived at a great sense of equanimity where there is no difference between what is inside the body and what is outside the body. The game is up.

This is something that every yogi is longing for, and this is something every human being is working towards, whether they are doing it consciously or not. In some way, they want to expand, and this is the Ultimate expansion. It is just that they are going towards the infinite in installments, which is a very long and impossible process. If you count – 1, 2, 3, 4 – you will only become endless counting. You will never reach the infinite. When one realizes the futility of this, he naturally turns inwards to do this – by untying the life process from the body.

*"Where the receptivity is in your hand and where the giving nature of the feet is – if these two things are connected – what you cannot achieve in years of sadhana, you may achieve in a moment."*

**Questioner: In India, it is a tradition to bow down at the feet of a Realized Being or a Guru. Is there any significance behind this?**

**Sadhguru:** In yoga, there is something called *Pada Shastra.* "*Pada*" means "the foot," particularly the soles of the feet. In many ways, all the switches to turn on almost everything in you are there in your feet, if you know how to do it.

When it comes to receiving, your hands are powerful instruments. If you are sensitive, if you touch anything with your hands, you will immediately know what it is. If you touch it with your shoulder or your back or the back of your head, you will not know what it is, but if you touch it with your hands, you will know what it is immediately, not just in terms of feeling and sensation – much deeper perception happens with your hands.

But if you want to give your energies to something, feet are very powerful instruments. At one time, we were teaching people how to manipulate the feet to create different states of experience – where to press if you want to relax somebody, if you want to make somebody blissful, if you want to make somebody loving. All the seven different chakras are manifest in your feet. If you know how to handle the feet, you can do many

*Body: The Greatest Gadget*

things with the whole system. Today, they call this reflexology, but they are talking only about health. Because we are interested in life, we talk in terms of experience.

About touching or holding feet, first of all, the one whose feet you are touching should have something to give; they should be in a certain level of energy. If you ask a pauper for a loan, it is no good. If you want to ask for a loan, you must ask somebody who has cash to dispense. If you go and ask for a loan from a bankrupt or a *kanjoos*,[8] there is no point. You know what a *kanjoos* means? Less "juice." You don't ask somebody who is juiceless or somebody who is stingy. You only ask somebody who is plentiful and willing to give.

You don't go and hold somebody's feet when he himself is bankrupt. If he is bursting with energies and he is willing to share, there is a certain way to connect, like a plug point. Plug points come in different ways. If you want to connect to that particular plug point, you need a particular kind of plug.

In many homes, you have a tradition or habit of touching the feet of your elders. Probably in South India it is gone, but in North India it is still very much there because of the Vedic culture. When they see a father, a mother, uncle, or anybody elder to them, the first thing they do is touch their feet. That is only to offer your respects to them, not to receive your uncle's energy! When you see a deity, there is another way of doing it. If you do *namaskar* or prostration to a powerful being, not spiritually evolved but powerful in his own way, there is another way of doing it. If you bow down to your Guru, there is another way of doing it. I don't want to go into these technologies. I can tell you the other three, but I don't want to tell you how to bow down to a Guru. Whichever way you feel, you do it that way because I don't want my legs pulled and held all the time!

---

8   A Hindi word meaning miser or scrooge.

Where the receptivity is in your hand and where the giving nature of the feet is – if these two things are connected – you may achieve in a moment what you cannot achieve in years of *sadhana*. It is with that hope that everybody is diving for the feet all the time, hoping that somewhere they may connect. Probably in western societies people understand falling at somebody's feet as a kind of subjugation or slavery. In the yogic tradition, we never thought feet were any less than the hands. It was never seen that one part of the body is less than the other. Wherever it works, that is how you do it.

When people from certain traditions come to me, I am amazed that these things have been taught to them from their childhood; they know exactly how to do it. Most other people are just doing it by their emotion. Sometimes they may get it right. So some people, just so that they don't make a mistake, touch all the parts! They know they have missed the technology, so they want to somehow connect. They will put their hands under his feet, it does not matter if the Guru falls and breaks his head – wherever it is, they want to get it. It is a treasure hunt.

That is the reason why whenever crowds increased, the Gurus always created an energy form and said, "Go bow down to that," to save their own feet. We can create an energy form to which you can bow down and receive, which is better. These are walking feet, but the energy forms cannot walk away from you. You can bow down as many times as you want per day, they cannot resist and it is okay.

*Body: The Greatest Gadget*

# The Illusion of Disease

## *"Disease and ailments happen fundamentally because somewhere your energy body is not functioning properly."*

**Questioner: Sadhguru, what are illness and disease? And how are they created? Are they creations of our minds?**

**Sadhguru:** When you say "disease," we have to first classify them into two basic categories. One set of diseases are infectious, you contract them from outside. Today you were negligent, you ate or drank something which was not hygienic, or you went close to somebody who had the flu and you caught an infection. For that, there are medicines and doctors. But there is another set of diseases, which are chronic ailments. These are something that the body creates.

The fundamental longing of the body is to survive and preserve itself. It is a very deep-rooted longing in this physical body; it wants to keep itself well. In spite of that, if it is creating diseases within itself, what could be wrong? It is because we are going on without understanding a few fundamentals. One thing is definitely the mind – psychosomatic diseases.

People who have had asthma for twenty-five years, come to the class,[9] and on the second or third day, it is gone. Just a little change in his attitude and it is gone. All along, every day he was creating this suffering for himself in the form of asthma. But if you tell him, "You are the one who is causing asthma," he will

---

9    Referring to the Isha Yoga Program.

think you are mad because according to his reasoning, he cannot understand, "Why will I cause asthma to myself? Why will I cause this suffering to myself? You are talking nonsense. How can I create asthma for myself? I want relief." But many times, people just drop the disease.

Some people may get rid of the disease with constant practice, but many have simply dropped the disease during the program. Within seven days, the *kriya* has not become powerful enough to cure a disease, but they simply drop it just by changing their attitude. They left their anger or hatred or jealousy, and suddenly the disease is gone.

If the mind is functioning in a certain way, it hampers the function of the energy. Whatever is happening in this body, in the form of creating, maintaining, and nurturing it, fundamentally depends on how your energy functions in this body. If your energy malfunctions for some reason, then a disease can manifest itself. In you, it may become one kind of disease. If the same malfunction happens in another person, it may become another kind of disease. On one level, some part of the body could be inherently weak in the system because it is weak in your parents. If a certain imbalance happens, depending upon what he has inherited, one person may get asthma, another may get diabetes. What type of imbalance you go through has a very deep *karmic* implication, because what we call as *karma* is a kind of software. It is a huge amount of impressions that we have taken into us which has become its own kind of software. This software has developed certain tendencies; it is tending to move in a particular way. Generally in the tradition, we call these, *vasanas*. "*Vasana*" literally means "smell." What kind of smell emanates from you depends on what kind of garbage you gathered, isn't it? If you have got a rotten fish in you, that is one kind of smell. If you spread this kind of smell around you, you will attract certain kinds of things. On some other day, if you smell another way, you will attract different kinds of things in the world. Depending upon what type of *vasanas* you have, accordingly you tend to move in certain ways and certain aspects in the world also tend to move towards you in a particular way.

Is this absolute? It is not absolute. If you become conscious, even if your smell is one way, you can go another way. But if you are not conscious, you naturally gravitate according to your tendencies. In the body, a certain manifestation of these tendencies can become disease. Because of certain tendencies, if the energy does not function properly in certain areas of the body, disease can happen.

Or, if you are under the influence of something else, then disease can happen. Even if your *karmic* structure is fine, your tendencies are good and taking you in the right directions, you kept your body well, but still, you may get a bad disease because you are under the influence of something else. Because this aspect also plays an important role, in ancient times, in this culture, they decided that every village and every town must have a temple.

This may be shocking for people, but actually, temples were never built as places of worship or prayer. In a temple, nobody leads you in prayer as it is done in a church; you are just left alone. You are supposed to sit there, that is all. These were energy centers which handle that dimension of the impact on your life which comes from the outside.

These impacts are like an infection, but not of virus or bacteria. Certain other tendencies – it could be a person, certain situations, certain spaces or evil intentions of people – affect the process of your life. So, every day, you go to a certain place where you do a little bit of cleansing for yourself – unless you become conscious and you have created your own inner ways to cleanse. If you don't have your own inner ways to cleanse your system, a temple was a public wash place for you to go and take off that element. It does not solve all your problems, but it takes off that element which comes into your life from external influences.

These are the different ways that you impair your energy system – either by your own *karmic* system, improper eating, improper attitudes, or the way your mind functions – your stress, your anxiety, your emotions, or other external influences – all this can impair the flow of energy in the system. All these aspects can be handled if you are doing a proper application of *kriyas*.[10]

There are different aspects of yoga. There are certain aspects of yoga which are not concerned about health; they are only concerned with taking you somewhere in your experience. There is a certain aspect of yoga which is concerned only with health. What you learn as the basic practice in Isha Yoga, one part of it is dedicated to health, another part to spiritual wellbeing. It is a good balance. We structured it this way because we are teaching this to people who are living in family and social situations.

In the United States, all the yoga institutes have turned into health institutes, which is not good. Health is only a lure. It has been made a part of yoga, but it is not the goal of yoga. Especially, in Western countries, people are going about as if health is the goal of life. Health is not the goal of life. There are more people on this planet healthy and miserable than unhealthy and miserable. At least if you are unhealthy, you have a good excuse for your misery. Health and misery, you have no excuse – that makes it all the more miserable.

---

10   Lit. Act, Rite. Refers to a certain class of yogic practices. Inward action as opposed to "karma" which means external action.

## *"Nobody who genuinely walks a spiritual path will ever attempt healing because it is a sure way of entangling yourself."*

**Questioner: Sadhguru, my father recently got into Reiki, and I have heard that Reiki, pranic healing and that sort of thing works on the *karmic* level and involves some sort of energy manipulation. My mother and I have asked him not to include us in these processes, but there has been a lot of conflict in the house because of this difference. Is there a way to shield myself from these things?**

**Sadhguru:** There are too many healers on the planet! A few years ago, one very popular healer from America came to Chennai. I don't know why healers from America are going to India, and healers from India are going to America. Why can't Indian healers heal in India, and American healers heal in America? They come here because people there know it does not work.

An American healer came to Chennai and there was a huge campaign and a big group of people gathered for healing on Chennai beach. People came and asked me, "Sadhguru, what is this healing? Should I go? I have this ailment, that ailment."

I said, "If you want, I will gather the addresses of all the hospitals on the planet and provide it to the healers. If you want to heal the sick, you must go to the hospital. Why the beach? I thought healthy people go there!"

*Body: The Greatest Gadget*

I am not saying there is nothing at all to it. Ninety percent of the time there is nothing to it, but ten percent of the time there could be something to it. When there is nothing to it, I am okay with it. Suppose someone sells nothing to you, he is just a smart business man and you are a little stupid, but no harm happens to you. You have the pleasure of shopping and he is doing business. Most of the time when you go to the mall, you only buy some "nothing," isn't it? You buy it, bring it home, and probably don't even open the cover. Whatever you bought just stays there many a time, because it is about the shopping, not about what you get. So, they are satisfying your shopping quest by selling nothing to you; there is no harm happening to you. But now, if he sells you something which causes you harm, that is worse than selling you nothing. Nothing is just a clean con-job. It only costs money, it does not cost life. But this "something" can cost life.

That ten percent of the time when something does happen, that is when the danger is. It is like Indian snakes. Ninety percent of them are non-poisonous. The bite is good, it gives you all the excitement – you go to the hospital and take anti-venom – but actually nothing happens. Even if you had just sat there, nothing would have happened. But when a snake from that ten percent bites you, that is when the real trouble is. This healing business is just like this. Ninety percent of the time they are just selling nothing. But that ten percent of the people who can do something, there is a danger attached to it, and it is unnecessary.

Today with modern medicine, you can handle almost all infectious diseases. When you use any kind of medicine, it is an attempt to change the chemistry of the body with an external input. Because of this, the system suffers in some way. On one level, the medicine cures you of the disease, but on another level it creates a kind of suffering. When it goes beyond a certain point, we say side-effects have manifested themselves because of the drug. But with any kind of drug or any kind of input, there will always be some disturbance to the system. If you are doing yogic practices, you can distinctly see that when you go on medication, your system is not the same. Whenever you try to influence the inner chemistry with external chemicals, there will be a disturbance. There is a price to pay, but it is needed because the disease is a bigger problem for you. But chronic ailments have not come to you from any external organism.

With chronic ailments, the disease is just the surface. The symptom that you notice is just the tip of the iceberg. And like the proverbial tip of the iceberg, it is only a small portion. The ailment that a person suffers is the symptom, which is all you notice, but it is just a small portion of the problem, which is elsewhere. Or in other words, the symptoms are like indicators.

Whenever somebody attempts any healing, they are always trying to remove the symptom, because that is what they consider as disease. If you take away the indicator, the root of the problem still exists. The indicator manifested itself on the physical body just to bring that root to your notice. Instead of taking notice of it and seeing what should be done about it, if you just wipe out the indicator, the root will take effect in a much more drastic way in your system. What was asthma can become a big accident or some other calamity in your life. It is possible.

If the root has to be removed, it cannot just be removed and dissolved like that. It has to be taken out and worked out in some way. These attempts to heal somebody are a very juvenile process, it is a very childish thing to do. People have not understood and experienced life in any great depth; they have seen life only in the physical dimension, so they believe that relieving a person of his physical pain at that moment is the greatest thing they can do. It is not so.

It is understandable that once the pain of the disease comes to you, you just want to be relieved, it does not matter how. But if you are beginning to feel life a little deeper than the physical

*Body: The Greatest Gadget*

body, you will see that how you get rid of your disease also matters.

Disease will go away if you dedicate enough attention to reorganizing your own energies. But you have to go through something. Just getting instant relief will relieve you in one way but bind you in some other way. Nobody who genuinely walks a spiritual path will ever attempt healing because it is a sure way of entangling yourself. Some of these things which have become famous around the globe today came from people who dropped out halfway through their spiritual process, after acquiring a little power. They wanted to use it and market themselves well.

At Isha, we teach you *sadhana* for liberation, to go beyond all your limitations. One can easily acquire such powers doing this *sadhana,* but we are taking a lot of care that you do not acquire any such thing. If you are on any live spiritual path, whoever is heading that place will always make sure that you never acquire any kinds of powers. We want to be ordinary, very ordinary – extra-ordinary. We don't have the disease of wanting to become special by doing something that others cannot do. It is not necessary. In trying to play God, in some way you want to do something that other human beings cannot do. This can lead to lots of entanglement. These things are a sideshow. In India, as you approach any temple, there will be shops on both sides with all kinds of trinkets. If you get too drawn to these trinkets, you will never reach the sanctum sanctorum. By the time you go there, the doors will be closed.

# "You are outnumbered ten to one."

**Questioner: When I visited the ashram, they served neem and turmeric balls for us to eat before doing our morning *sadhana*. What is the significance of this?**

**Sadhguru**: Neem is very cleansing for your system. The neem stick is good, you know, it awakens lots of people. In India, if you are acting a little funny and possessed, they can beat the devil out of you with the neem stick! If you have any kind of infection, they would always put you on a bed of neem leaves because it is a great energizer and cleanser of the system. The leaf has tremendous medicinal properties and very strong *pranic*[11] reverberations – and it is bitter enough to get the devil out of you!

A neem leaf is the most complex leaf that you can find on the planet, and it has particular benefits in opening up the system. For people who have come from the West, one of the biggest problems for you in India is you will have stomach infections. Just about anything, which the Indians think is fantastic, will keep you permanently in the toilet, because the world is full of bacteria. The body is full of bacteria. In a normal sized body, you have approximately 10 trillion human cells, but you have over 100 trillion bacteria. You are outnumbered one to ten. There are more creatures living in you than you imagine. Most of these bacteria are very helpful to us. Without them we cannot exist,

---

11   Relating to prana, or the vital life energies.

but some of them can cause trouble to us. If you put neem into the system it destroys the troublesome bacteria in the intestinal region.

Neem has many incredible benefits, but one of the most important things is that it kills cancerous cells. When I say cancerous cells, every one of our bodies has cancerous cells, but they are disorganized, they are all over the place. For some reason, if you create certain situations in the body, they will get organized. From petty crime to organized crime – serious problem, isn't it? There are petty criminals everywhere in every town. Here and there they will do a little pick-pocketing, no problem. But if fifty of them get organized in a city, then suddenly the whole atmosphere in the city will change. These fifty guys together can do such things that it will become dangerous for you to step onto the street. That is all that is happening in the body. There are cancerous cells running around. If they are loafing around by themselves, no problem. If they all meet in one place and hit it off, then it is a problem. The thing is to keep breaking them up, here and there killing a few guys, before they gang up. Having neem every day does that; it keeps the number of cancerous cells in the body within a certain percentage, where it does not really gang up against the system. So it is a very important thing to consume neem.

If you eat neem, even mosquitos may not bite you. If you smear yourself with neem paste just before bath, let it dry for some time and just wash it off with water, it is a cleanser by itself – all the bacteria on the outside will die. Or you can take a few neem leaves and put it in the water, leave it there overnight and have bath with it.

It is important that there are no excess levels of bacteria. Without bacterial activity you cannot exist. But if the bacterial levels are excessive, you will feel "down" because the defense mechanism spends too much energy dealing with them. By using neem in a variety of ways, you manage the bacteria in such a way that you do not have to spend the body's energy in managing it.

Turmeric is one substance which not only works on the physiology, but also works on the energy system. It creates a certain purification process in the blood, body and energy system. You can use this as a purificatory substance even from outside. If you just take a small pinch of turmeric, put it into a bucket full of water and pour it over your body, you will see the body will be vibrant and glowing. Keeping the blood pure and the blood chemistry in a certain balance will definitely happen with regular consumption of turmeric. It purifies the blood and brings a certain translucence to your energies.

*"If you want to meditate, your alertness must be not of the mind alone, but of your very energy."*

**Questioner: Sadhguru, when I do *sadhana*, I am finding myself dozing off. I thought this was due to tiredness, but whenever I close my eyes and meditate, I fall asleep. How can I stay awake?**

Sadhguru: First, let us understand what sleep is about. If sleep is invading your life anytime of the day, you must first check your basic health and see if there is something wrong with your system. When you are physically unwell, you will tend to sleep much more than normal – the body wants to rest.

The second thing is the food that you eat. Consuming at least a certain amount of vegetarian material, particularly in uncooked condition, is very important for your general wellbeing. When you cook food, a large volume of *prana* is destroyed. That is one of the reasons why a certain amount of lethargy settles into the body. If you just eat a certain amount of live food, apart from many other benefits, one thing that will immediately happen is your sleep quota will go down dramatically.

Essentially, your alertness depends on how keenly you manage your energies. If you want to meditate, your alertness must be not of the mind alone, but of your very energy. To assist this, generally, for people who are on the yogic path, it is said that you should eat only twenty-four mouthfuls, and you must chew every mouthful at least twenty-four times. Now your food will be pre-digested in your mouth before it goes in, and it will not cause dullness.

If you do this during your evening meal and then sleep in the night, you will easily wake up at three-thirty in the morning, and you can meditate. In the yogic systems, this time is called the *Brahma Muhurtam*. It is an ideal time to wake up, because at that time, there is an extra support from nature itself for your *sadhana*. If you take a bath and keep your hair wet, you will easily stay awake and alert through your *sadhana* until eight o'clock. If you eat just twenty-four morsels in your morning meal, you will definitely not feel sleepy until dinnertime. After one-and-a-half to two hours, you will be hungry, and that is the best way to be. Just because the stomach is empty, you do not have to put food. Just drink water and you will stay alert and energetic throughout the day. Your system will learn to use the food you have eaten well, rather than simply wasting it. Economically and ecologically it is good for the world, and good for your health – you may never fall sick if you eat like this.

*Body: The Greatest Gadget*

# "When it comes to food, experiment with different foods and see how your body feels after eating the food."

**Questioner: What role does food play in keeping the body healthy? Some people say vegetarian is the way to go, but others say you cannot stay healthy without some meat in the diet. It is really confusing...**

**Sadhguru:** What kind of food you eat should depend not on what you think about it, or on your values and ethics, but on what the body wants. Food is about the body. When it comes to food, don't ask your doctors or your nutrition experts; they keep changing their opinion every five years. Do experiment with different foods and see how your body feels after eating. If your body feels very agile, energetic and nice, that means the body is "happy." If the body feels lethargic and needs to be pumped up with caffeine or nicotine to stay awake, the body is not happy.

If you listen to your body, it will clearly tell you what kind of food it is happy with. But right now, you are listening to your mind, which keeps lying to you all the time. Hasn't it lied to you before? Today it tells you this is it. Tomorrow it makes you feel like a fool for what you believed yesterday. So don't go by your mind. You just have to learn to listen to your body.

Every animal and every creature knows what to eat and what not to. The human species is supposed to be the most intelligent on the planet, but they don't even know what to eat. It takes a certain attention to learn to listen to your body, then you will know what to eat.

In terms of the quality of food that is entering you, vegetarian food is definitely far better for the system than non-vegetarian. We are not looking at it from a moral standpoint. We are just looking at what is suitable for the system – we try to eat foods which would make us comfortable in the body. Whether you want to run your business, study, or do any activity properly, it is extremely important that your body is at ease. The kind of food with which your body would be most at ease and would get nourishment from most effortlessly, is the kind of food we should eat.

Just experiment and see, when you eat vegetarian food in its "live" form, what a difference it will make. The idea is to eat as much live food as possible – whatever can be consumed in its aliveness. A live cell has everything to sustain life. If you consume a live cell, the sense of health in your system will be very different from anything that you have known. When we cook foods, it destroys the life in it. Eating foods after the life in it has been destroyed does not give the same amount of life energy to the system. But when you eat live foods, it brings a different level of aliveness in you. If one eats lots of sprouts, fruit, and whatever vegetables that can be eaten in a live condition – if you bring in at least thirty to forty percent live food – it will sustain the life within you very well.

On another level, it has become normal in the so-called civilized world to eat food which was cooked three days ago. In India, the moment people start following the western culture, the first thing they will do is start taking stale food. Ask a local, illiterate villager, he will not touch stale food. In India, if somebody eats old food, we say he is like a beggar; but now, all the well-to-do in the world are taking stale food. If your body has to maintain a certain level of energy, it is very important that the food should not get matured – you say it has gone bad, but actually it is maturing. Every moment, bacteria are culturing the food slowly. You do not realize this till it stinks, but it is happening from the very first moment you cook it.

Above all, the food that you eat is life. It is other forms of life that we are eating – another life form is giving up its life for yours. If we can eat with enormous gratitude for all the living things which give up their life to sustain ours, then the food will behave in a very different way within you.

*Body: The Greatest Gadget*

# The Five-cornered Game

***"The five elements of earth, water, air, fire and space, are the basis of this body, the basis of this planet, and the basis of the whole creation."***

Flowers can make nectar and fragrance, and of course color. A bee can build a wonderful hive and fill it with sweetness – it is guarded by a bitter sting. Birds can sing. Human beings can do all this, and human beings can also realize that all these things – producing color, fragrance, sweetness – are being done pretty well by other creatures, and see how to go beyond this.

I am not against the sweetness of life, nor against the color or fragrance. But even if we do not do any of these things, nothing is really lost because nature is doing it much better than us. If musicians stop singing, nothing will be lost because if we listen carefully, every leaf, every tree, even the very breeze is humming its own rhythm if you are willing to listen. If painters stop painting, nothing will be lost. People, instead of wowing imitations, would probably start looking at the original.

It is good that human beings can do all this because in the evolutionary process of life, human beings are placed in a position of intelligence and capability where we can be a composite expression of all creatures. Many human beings though, have not produced the kind of sweetness that a bee is capable of producing. They are armed with a sting worse than the bee's, yet they have no sweetness to protect. Still, the most important thing is that a human being is capable of rising above this whole play.

The five elements of earth, water, air, fire and space, are the basis of this body, the basis of this planet and the basis of

*Body: The Greatest Gadget*

the whole creation. These are the five ingredients with which creation is made. If these five elements play a certain kind of game, it is called mud. If the game they play is a little different, the same thing becomes food. If they play another kind of game, it becomes human. If they play yet a different kind of game, it becomes Divine. Everything that you see in creation is just a juggling of these five things.

It is a five-cornered game – just five ingredients. Even if you want to make *sambar*, you need seventeen ingredients. But with just five ingredients, what a creation! Five is not a complicated number. Human intelligence should be capable of juggling five. Just with five, it is such a complex game, or so it seems. When something seems so phenomenally complex and you dive into it, and find it is just a juggling of five things, it becomes a joke; a cosmic joke. Once you know something is one big joke, you refuse to play.

Recently, I was at the New York airport. There was a man, probably over sixty years of age, with a long beard (not me, I was not looking in the mirror!). He looked at me and nodded. I also nodded. Then I saw that he was wearing a t-shirt where it was boldly written, "I don't play anymore." I know in what context he meant this; the old guy still wants to boast about his youthful adventures. But, I saw it in a different way. All yogis are actually wearing the same t-shirt: "I don't play anymore," but in a completely different context. It is because they realize that it is such a simple game projecting itself to be so complex – magnified billions of times.

A few years ago, I was driving up a mountain in India, and as I was approaching it, I could see almost half the mountain was ablaze! It was misty and I saw the whole place was on fire, but I am known to always be driving into hot places. I was driving a car with flammable fuel, so I didn't want to drive into it, but I continued to drive, carefully watching. However far I went, it seemed to be a little further away. Then I realized that I had actually driven through all the places which looked as if they were on fire from the bottom of the mountain.

When I reached the actual place of the fire, I saw a broken down truck. The driver and two other people who were there had made a small fire because there was a chill in the air. That little fire, because of the mist, was getting magnified millions of times and from down below, it looked like the whole mountain was on fire. That phenomenon really freaked me. It was just a little fire that people had created for warmth, but every particle of mist was magnifying it and the whole place looked like it was on fire.

Creation is just like that – hugely magnified. Those who looked at it closely, realized this and said, "There is no need to look at the magnified version. Look at this little piece of life that you call 'myself' – that's all." The rest of the cosmos is just a magnified projection of a little thing that is happening – just five elements.

"If you know how to organize these five elements properly within yourself, there is nothing more to life. In terms of health, wellbeing, perception, knowing and enlightenment – everything is handled if only you know how to keep these five elements properly."

In yoga, we have devised a scientific process of becoming free from the five elements, called *bhuta shuddhi*. This is the most basic practice in yoga. "*Bhuta*" means the *pancha bhutas*, or the five elements; "*shuddhi*" means to cleanse. If you cleanse the elements sufficiently, then you attain to a state which we refer to as *bhuta siddhi*, which means you have a certain mastery over your five elements.

It is from this basic practice of *bhuta shuddhi* that various other practices have evolved in the yogic system – they are just a small extraction from this fundamental process. In Southern India, they even built five major temples for the five elements.

*Body: The Greatest Gadget*

These temples were created for specific types of *sadhana*. To become free from the water element, you go to that particular temple and do one kind of *sadhana*. To become free from air, you go to another temple and do another kind of *sadhana*. Like this, for all the five elements, five wonderful temples were infused with the kind of energy which assists that type of *sadhana*. Yogis used to travel from temple to temple, continuing their *sadhana* from one to the other.

The fundamental process of yoga is towards attaining to a state of *bhuta siddhi,* so that the life process is no longer an accidental process, it is not a compulsive reaction to the situations in which we exist – it is a conscious process. Once the life process is a conscious process, to be pleasant and blissful is natural, and to move towards liberation is inevitable.

The air that you breathe, the water that you drink, the food that you eat, the land that you walk upon, and the fire of life in the form of the life force – if you keep these controlled and focused, then health, wellbeing and success in the world are assured.

It is my endeavor to create various devices which will allow people to make this happen for themselves in such a way that the very way you exist is a *Pancha Bhuta Aradhana.*[12] The way this body, this physical self exists here should be in adoration of the five elements. One can use this for their physical wellbeing, for their worldly success, and at the same time, it can be a great stepping stone for one's ultimate liberation too.

---

12   A process conducted every month on Shivaratri at the Dhyanalinga Yogic Temple, where the qualities of each of the five elements are offered to the Dhyanalinga and in turn, the five elements are purified in the system of those present.

*"You are just a small outcrop of this earth. Right now, you are an outcrop that prances around. As a little blade of grass has shot out of the earth, you are also like that – a little mobile, that is all."*

**Questioner: Why is it that yogis choose to live in mountains and not in the plains?**

**Sadhguru:** Just to avoid people like you, that's all! Why do they choose mountains? Why not plains, valleys, or coasts? Mean sea level would be much more comfortable, because you could live with bare minimum. A *sanyasi* on a beach would be just fine, isn't it? No extra clothing needed, no problem. It would be very easy. On the mountains, it is very different. It is very difficult, but they still chose mountains because a mountain is a place where earth has risen to reach out to you, so that you don't escape.

A yogi is always looking for small enclosures. A yogi is somebody who is completely re-creating life within himself and outside of himself. He always wants a place which is small in size, which is compact, where he can create his own kind of energy and his own kind of world. If you look at it from your perception, the cave is just a small hole to crawl into, but in his experience it is bigger than the world, because time and space is an illusion created by your mind. What is small, what is big, what is now, what is then, is all the illusion of the mind. Once a person has transcended this limitation, he can create a whole universe in his cave.

*Body: The Greatest Gadget*

Mountains are a place where earth has risen up in some way. If you bore a hole into the ground, dig a well, and try to stay in it, it will not be comfortable for many reasons. Slowly, you must become a frog because it will fill up. But a mountain cave is in the mountain itself. It is the only place where you are enveloped with earth on all sides. That is the reason why yogis always chose mountains, not valleys, not plains, because for their work, they want to be surrounded by earth. That is why we have built the Dhyanalinga temple like a mound of earth. It is surrounded by earth – that is the nearest thing that we could do.

When I went to Kentucky in the United States, we went to a place called Mammoth Caves.[13] If you go inside, ten to twenty thousand people can easily sit inside. It is a huge natural cave. There are about ten acres of sitting space, or probably more. When I saw it, I thought if we had a cave like this, we could have consecrated it so powerfully. The nearest thing that we could build, surrounded by earth, is the dome of the Dhyanalinga temple. Dhyanalinga is surrounded by earth because that is the best way to keep it.

A yogi wants to keep himself in that kind of situation where he is surrounded by earth. A mountain is the only natural topography which offers certain opportunities. It is a constant reminder for the body that the play of elements in the earth and in this body is not different.

You are just a small outcrop of this earth. Right now you are an outcrop that prances around. When the earth decides to suck you in, you just become a small mound. As a little blade of grass has shot out of the earth, you are also like that – a little mobile, that's all. You may believe yourself to be something else, but that is all you are. The body should never forget what it is. If it

---

13    Mammoth Caves, a part of the Mammoth Cave National Park in Kentucky, is the longest cave system known in the world.

forgets, it starts making fanciful demands – "I want this, I want to be like that." We always want to keep it close to the earth to remind the body – "You are just a piece of this." If you constantly remind it, then it remembers its place. Yogis always chose to live in the mountains because there, the body is suddenly strongly reminded of its mortality – not a mental or intellectual reminder – but a physical reminder.

The space between life and death is so flimsy. That space or that line is narrowed in the mountains. If you realize the mortality of who you are, if you are constantly aware that you will die, if your physical body is aware that it is not permanent, that it is going to be sucked into this earth one day – and it could be today – now your spiritual search is unwavering. A yogi wants to be constantly reminded of his or her mortality, so that their spiritual search does not waver at all.

Being in touch with the earth also has many other aspects to it. The elemental play of the body happens in a different way when it is in touch with the earth.

Have you heard of yogis being buried neck deep in the earth? The ignorant around them might have thought that they were trying to perform a feat and prove something. But this is not to perform a feat; they are just reorganizing their system. Today, you are unwilling to do that, so you go to an expensive spa and have a mud bath, but one of the things that can be done is to bury yourself for a few hours a day. It actually helps. If you are not willing to be buried, at least smear the earth upon the body. By just being in touch with the earth, the system will start reorganizing itself. The body is reminded of its own nature in a very fundamental way, and that reminder must be on all the time.

In the Yoga Center in India, we have a Rejuvenation Center. Earlier we used to call this the yogic hospital. So, when I was in the United States, I had been talking about all the miraculous cures that are happening in the yogic hospital and a few doctors from United States landed up at the ashram. They went around the ashram, looking for the yogic hospital. They did not find any beds or patients, so they said, "This is rubbish! Sadhguru has been talking to us about a yogic hospital and there is no yogic hospital." When I met them they asked, "Where is the yogic hospital?" They were completely put off.

I said, "Right now there are about seventy patients with us. It is just that I don't let them lie down on the bed and languish there. I just put them to work, particularly in the garden."

One of the fundamental things is they must walk bare feet for two hours on the earth and put their hands into the earth. That is the basic early morning treatment for them. So I said, "Just go out in the garden and ask them what is their ailment, they will explain why they are here." Because it is common knowledge, even among the medical fraternity, that your body's defence mechanism works at its best when you are physically active. If you just lie down, the bacterial level in the body goes up phenomenally, and your body's ability to handle itself comes down dramatically. Horizontal positions reduce the whole body's integrity. This is the reason why people are sitting in vertical postures for hours and hours, because they are reorganizing their system.

If the body is deteriorating for some reason, if you come in contact with the earth, there are many *sadhanas* that can be done to heal it. If you do the right kind of *sadhana,* if you are in touch with earth, even if you just walk barefoot in your garden every day for an hour where there are no ticks and thorns, within a week's time your sense of health will be greatly enhanced. Just try this and see. Get off your high cot, just sleep on the floor. You can clearly notice that there will be a great sense of health in your body.

This is the reason why in the Indian tradition, we were always told to eat on the floor and sleep on the floor. Whatever we do, we sit on the floor, not because we cannot afford a cot, but simply because in the first one-and-a-half feet from the Earth, the thickness of the *pranic* vibration is a lot more than it is above. As it goes up, it becomes thinner and thinner. That is why even if we place a deity, we don't place him on a great altar, we place him very close to Earth. We built very large temples, such massive structures, so it would not be difficult for us to raise a one-hundred foot platform and put him there, but he is always put low down, almost to the ground or slightly up. This is simply because the *pranic* vibrations are best, low down.

That is why all spiritual beings generally move to the mountains or caves, though the conditions are not comfortable, because it gives you a closer contact with the earth. If you make a hole or a cave in it, the earth is on all sides.

*Body: The Greatest Gadget*

*"Water is one thing that is freaking the scientific community. They cannot understand what water is because it is one of the few substances which contracts when you heat it and expands when you cool it; it is one of the few things which exists on earth in all the three states of being solid, liquid and gaseous, and it is the very basis of our life."*

**Questioner: Sadhguru, what do you mean by existing here as an adoration of five elements? How do we bring this adoration within ourselves?**

**Sadhguru**: Changing the quality of the elements or determining how these elements behave within us is very much within the human mind and consciousness. The science and technology of this was explored to its fullest depth and transmitted through the ages in this culture, but in the last hundred years, because of a very upstart-ish attitude towards life, we have dropped many things. If we fall back on the knowledge bank that we have in this country, it could be the greatest asset – not only for this nation's wellbeing, but for the world's wellbeing as well. All the methods coming from the West are generally useful only in the short-term. Everything is just use and throw, including the human being. And we have come to this kind of conclusion – because of political and other kinds of dominance – that if something comes from the West it becomes science; if it comes from the East it becomes superstition.

Many of the things that your grandmothers would have once told you, are today being discovered in top scientific laboratories as "great" discoveries about human nature. Everything that they are saying after billion-dollar research studies, we have already said in our culture, because this is not a culture which has evolved out of compulsions of living. This is a culture which was evolved consciously by sages and saints, seeing how you should sit, how you should stand, and how you should eat. It was designed for what is best for human wellbeing, and there is immense scientific value in it.

Today, particularly in the last few years, a phenomenal amount of research has gone into water and the potential of water. This started off inadvertently because of the way the availability of usable water in the world is reducing per person. In India for example, today, an average Indian has only twenty percent of the potable water he had in 1947. They say by 2025, we will have only seven percent of what we had in 1947 per person. Because of this, a lot of research has gone into water. Experiments are being conducted which scientists think are phenomenal, and can change the very way we live on this planet.

One thing scientists are saying is that water has memory. Like a fluid memory bank, water remembers whatever it comes in touch with. In today's water supply system, water is pumped forcefully through a pipe, and it may take fifty bends before coming to your tap. By the time the water lands in your house, they are saying that sixty percent of it will be poisonous – not chemically, but because its molecular structure will have changed. It may not be contaminated the way you normally look at it in terms of bacteria, but just the force of travel is making the molecular structure change in such a way that it is no longer beneficial, perhaps even poisonous. If you hold this water in a copper vessel and keep it there for ten or twelve hours, the damage will undo itself. But if you drink it from the tap straight away, you are drinking a certain volume of poison. People live like this and they wonder, "Why did I get cancer? Why did I get this?" You live without any sensitivity towards life, without taking care of the ingredients which build you, and you expect everything to be okay.

*Body: The Greatest Gadget*

It has been found that without changing the chemical composition of water, you can rearrange the molecular arrangement so that the water will behave in a completely different way. For example, if I take a glass of water in my hand, look at it in a certain way and give it to you, wellbeing will come to you. If I look at it another way and give it to you, you will fall sick tonight.

Your grandmother used to tell you, "You should not drink water or eat food from just anybody's hands. You must always receive it from people who love you and care for you. You should not consume things from anywhere and everywhere." When your grandmother told you this, it was superstition. If you hear about it from scientists in the US, then you will take it seriously. This is a kind of slavery.

In this culture, we have always known that water has memory. What you call as *theerth*[14] is just this. You have seen how people struggle to get that one drop of *theerth* from the temple. Even if you are a billionaire, you still die for that one drop of water because you want to take in water which has the memory of the Divine.

If you go to any traditional home in Tamil Nadu – this was so everywhere in the country, but in other places it has largely been lost – you will see that water is stored in a certain way, either in brass or copper vessels. Every morning, they will wash it with tamarind, apply some *vibhuti*[15] and put some *kumkum*[16] on it, and do *pooja* for it. Only then do they store water in it, and only from that they will drink, because they always knew that water

---

14    Water which has been blessed or energized by a particular deity, temple, or shrine. It is often offered in the main shrine of ancient Indian temples and is said to carry the blessings of the idol there.

15    Sacred, consecrated ash. Applied to different parts of the body to make one more sensitive to subtle life forces. Application to the upper chakras, activates the chakras and makes them more receptive.

16    Vermillion or red powder made of turmeric and lime. Worn at the point of the third eye on the forehead.

has memory. They knew that the kind of container you keep it in, and how you treat it, influences how it behaves within you.

Let me tell you of an incident that happened. A few years ago, I went to a South Indian home, and here the first sign of hospitality is that they bring water for you to drink. So the lady in the house brought water for me. I looked at her face, and she was looking like Kali because her husband wanted to come for a ninety-day program with me. She is a nice lady, but that day she was like Kali. So when she brought the water, I said, "Amma, today you are like a Kali. I have no need to drink this water. I am not in such a desperate condition, okay?"

She said, "It is good water, only." She was saying it was not poisoned.

So I said, "It is good water, but the way you are, I don't need to drink this water."

If Sadhguru comes to your house and refuses to drink water, that is not a simple thing in a South Indian family. A drama started unfolding. Then I knew if I leave it like this, the drama will become very big.

So I said to her, "Take a sip of the water."

She thought I was using her as a food taster, and she drank it and said, "It is good."

I asked her to give me the water, and just held it in my hand for a minute and gave it to her. "Now you drink it."

She drank it, burst into tears and started crying, "Oh, it is sweet, it is sweet."

I said, "That is all life is. If you are in a certain way, everything turns sweet. If you are in a certain other way, everything will become bitter in your life."

If with just a thought or a look, you can turn the water in a vessel sweet, then with the right kind of attitude, focus, and attention towards it, can't you turn sweet the water in this vessel of the body? If you turn that water sweet, you are seventy-two percent sweet.

*Body: The Greatest Gadget*

*"If you get cooperation from akash, life will happen in magical ways. An intelligence that you have never thought possible will become yours."*

Modern science is beginning to recognize that there is something called as *akashik* intelligence. That is, empty space has a certain intelligence. How this *akashik* intelligence behaves with you – whether this intelligence works for you or works against you – will determine the nature of your life. Whether you are a blessed being or one who is going to be knocked around for the rest of your life simply depends on your ability – either consciously or unconsciously – to be able to get the cooperation of this larger intelligence, which is functioning.

It is improper to call *akash* or space, the fifth element because it is *the* element. All the other four just play upon it; the fundamental element is *akash*. It is in the lap of this boundless space that these four elements play the game. We are sitting here on a round, spinning planet in the solar system. It is all held in place only by *akash*. You are sitting in your place not because of yourself, you are sitting in your place only because *akash* is holding you in place. It is *akash* which is holding this earth, this solar system, this galaxy and the whole cosmos in place – and no strings attached, just see! Just held like that.

If you know how to get the cooperation of *akash* into your life, this will be a blessed life. One simple process you can do for this is, after sunrise, before the sun crosses an angle of thirty degrees, look up at the sky once and bow down to *akash* for holding you in the place today. After the sun crosses thirty degrees, sometime during the day – anytime – look up and bow down again. After the sun sets, once again look up and bow down, not to some god up there, just to the empty space for holding you in the place for today. Just do this. Life will change dramatically.

Have you noticed, even Tendulkar looks up? It is not just him, right from ancient times, when man achieved something in great moments of success, he looks up because unknowingly there is a realization. Some of them may be looking up for the *uperwaala*,[17] but mostly, when you hit a peak experience, have you noticed, even without your awareness, your body looks up in gratitude? Somewhere there is recognition; there is an intelligence here which recognizes that.

Do this process consciously three times a day. If you get cooperation from *akash,* life will happen in magical ways. An intelligence that you have never thought possible will become yours.

---

17   Refers to the Hindi word for God, "the one above."

*Body: The Greatest Gadget*

*"There are certain patterns running in your aura. If you run fire along those tracks, suddenly you feel bright and clear."*

Have you noticed that when you have a shower, when you let water go over you, you are not just cleaning the skin, something else also gets cleaned? Let us say you are feeling very angry or agitated, and all kinds of things are happening within you. If you just have a shower, you may feel that all the nonsense has washed off.

A shower is not just about cleaning the skin of your body; you can cleanse the aura too, to some extent. The aura is the subtle manifestation of everything that you are. If you look at one's aura, you clearly know his physical health, his mental health, his *karmic* structure – in a way his past and present, and if he is stupid, even his future. Only if you are stupid we can tell your future, otherwise we can only tell your past.

The aura is a certain manifestation of yourself, a subtler manifestation in the physical body. It is good to keep it clean. Isn't it good to keep your body clean? Even if you don't understand, somebody sitting next to you understands that it is good! It is good to keep your body, mind and everything that is you, clean. I am not trying to teach you sanitation or hygiene. What I am saying is that if you want to take anything to a higher possibility, the first thing is to purify. Without purification, you cannot do anything better than the way it is right now.

There are many methods you can learn to purify your body and mind, from doing *kriyas* to eating properly. Aura is a manifestation, it is not a presence by itself, but if you are doing *sadhana* and you are improving your system, what you manifested yesterday or what you manifested ten years ago may be still hanging around you and not allowing you to become what you want to be. That can be cleansed.

Just as you take a shower with water, similarly, you can give yourself a wind bath. Suppose there is a gentle breeze blowing. If you wear thin clothes and stand in that wind, after some time you feel so clean and transparent. Wind can do that. It should be at just the right velocity, feel, temperature and everything. If it is right, wind just cleanses you. That is a wind bath. We can also give you a mud bath. If you go to the Rejuvenation Center,[18] they give you a mud bath. Similarly, we can give you a fire bath.

What is being done in the Bhairavi temple[19] is a fire bath. Of course, you cannot pour it over your body, you can just touch the aura of your body in a certain way. There are certain patterns running in your aura. If you run fire along those tracks, suddenly you feel bright and clear. People from Indian origin clearly know this. In your homes, your grandmothers were taking off *drishti*[20] for you – aura cleansing. Maybe some of your grandmothers knew exactly how to do it, and some of them did not know, so with ignorance they simply did something. If it is properly done, it will work wonderfully well. Even if it is done without proper

---

18    The Isha Rejuvenation Center is a holistic health spa situated at the Isha Yoga Center.

19    Linga Bhairavi Devi is a fierce and exuberant form of the Mother Goddess. The ritual of "fire bath" is offered in the Linga Bhairavi Temple near the Isha Yoga Center.

20    Lit. vision. Here, it refers to the "evil eye" – said to inflict people and especially young children, through the negative thought and intentions and intentions of people around them.

*Body: The Greatest Gadget*

understanding, it still works partially. Any number of times, people might have noticed that when children are sick, they get better if just a little fire bath is done. It does things to the system.

What is being given in the temple is *Klesha Nashana Kriya*, a process which destroys impurities. In English it is called aura cleansing. It is to take away the impurities from the aura so that the body breathes and feels better in terms of health, wellbeing, and mental balance.

# *"If one has mastery over the five elements, the body can even be dematerialized."*

If one has mastery over the five elements, the body can even be dematerialized – that means, it is no more. There are any number of yogis who have done this.

There was a particular yogi by the name of Vallalar Ramalinga Adigalar, from Tamil Nadu. One day, he went into a room, and he never came out. People waited for him to come out. Then they broke the doors open and went inside. Vallalar was not there, all that was left was a bit of water on the floor. Instead of giving nature the trouble of recycling him into the earth, he just dematerialized himself. Such things have happened, and such things are still happening.

Recently, someone who has the Linga Bhairavi Yantra[21] in their home, found a small pool of water around the *yantra*. This was kept in a place where there was no way for any kind of water to come, but they found lots of water upon and around the *yantra*. It is just that one life which does not belong to that family made use of this energy to completely dematerialize and disappear; all that was left was a little pool of water. Many yogis have demonstrated this level of elemental integrity. They leave the body in such a way that no body is left, no bones are left, only a little bit of water is left. This is the peak of elemental integrity, where all the elements are integrated to such a point that it all becomes space.

---

21    Unique and powerful energy forms, designed by Sadhguru, which carry the energy of Linga Bhairavi Devi.

# *Sadhguru*

Yogi, mystic, and visionary, Sadhguru is a spiritual master with a difference. An arresting blend of profundity and pragmatism, his life and work serve as a reminder that yoga is not an esoteric discipline from an outdated past, but a contemporary science, vitally relevant to our times. Probing, passionate and provocative, insightful, logical and unfailingly witty, Sadhguru's talks have earned him the reputation of a speaker and opinion-maker of international renown.

With speaking engagements that take him around the world, he is widely sought after by prestigious global forums to address issues as diverse as human rights, business values, and social, environmental and existential issues. He has been a delegate to the United Nations Millennium World Peace Summit, a member of the World Council of Religious and Spiritual Leaders and Alliance for New Humanity, a special invitee to the Australian Leadership Retreat, Tallberg Forum, Indian Economic Summit 2005-2008, as well as a regular at the World Economic Forum in Davos.

With a celebratory engagement with life on all levels, Sadhguru's areas of active involvement encompass fields as diverse as architecture and visual design, poetry and painting, ecology and horticulture, sports and music. He is the author and designer of several unique buildings and consecrated spaces at the Isha Yoga Center, which have wide attention for their combination of intense sacred power with strikingly innovative eco-friendly aesthetics.

Listeners have been ubiquitously impressed by his astute and incisive grasp of current issues and world affairs, as well as his unerringly scientific approach to the question of human wellbeing. Sadhguru is also the founder of Isha Foundation, a non-profit organization dedicated to the wellbeing of the individual and the world for the past three decades. Isha Foundation does not promote any particular ideology, religion, or race, but transmits inner sciences of universal appeal.

http://sadhguru.org
http://www.youtube.com/sadhguru

# *Isha Foundation*

Isha Foundation is a non-profit human-service organization, founded by Sadhguru and supported by over two million volunteers in over 150 centers worldwide. Recognizing the possibility of each person to empower another, Isha Foundation has created a massive movement that is dedicated to address all aspects of human wellbeing, without ascribing to any particular ideology, religion or race.

From its powerful yoga programs to its inspiring projects for society and environment, Isha activities are designed to create an inclusive culture that is the basis for global harmony and progress.

Isha Foundation is also involved in several path-breaking outreach initiatives: Action for Rural Rejuvenation (ARR) enhances the quality of rural life through healthcare and disease prevention, community revitalization, women empowerment, the creation of sustainable livelihoods, and yoga programs. Isha Vidhya empowers rural children with quality education. Project GreenHands (PGH) initiates mass tree planting and creates a culture of care for the environment to keep this planet liveable for future generations. The project was awarded the Government of India's highest environmental accolade, the Indira Gandhi Paryavaran Puraskar.

Isha's unique approach in cultivating human potential has gained worldwide recognition and reflects in Isha Foundation's special consultative status with the Economic and Social Council (ECOSOC) of the United Nations.

The Foundation is headquartered at the Isha Yoga Center, set in the lush rainforest at the base of the Velliangiri Mountains in southern India, and at the Isha Institute of Inner-sciences on the spectacular Cumberland Plateau in central Tennessee, USA.

http://www.ishafoundation.org
http://blog.ishafoundation.org

*Body: The Greatest Gadget*

# Isha Yoga

At the core of the Isha Institute of Inner-sciences' activities is a customized system of yoga called Isha Yoga. Isha Yoga distills powerful, ancient yogic methods for a modern person, creating peak physical, mental, and emotional wellbeing. This basis of total wellbeing accelerates inner growth, allowing each individual to tap the wealth of vibrant life within oneself. Sadhguru's introductory program, Inner Engineering, introduces Shambhavi Mahamudra a simple but powerful *kriya* (inner energy process) for deep inner transformation.

The uniqueness of Isha Yoga is that it is offered as a science. It draws on the ancient yogic principle that the body is the temple of the spirit and that good health is fundamental to personal and spiritual development. Scientifically structured, it promotes beneficial changes in one's inner chemistry to accelerate the release of physical, mental and emotional blocks and produce a life-transforming impact of profound experience, clarity and boundless energy.

Isha Yoga involves a combination of carefully selected purificatory and preparatory practices, including a series of dynamic breathing techniques and meditation in simple sitting postures. The practices that are taught do not demand physical agility or previous experience of yoga. They integrate seamlessly into one's daily life, allowing one to function at the optimum level, making peace and joy one's natural way of being.

Thus, individuals, regardless of their personal situations or backgrounds, have the possibility to integrate a powerful spiritual process into their lives.

http://www.ishayoga.org

# Inner Engineering

Inner Engineering is offered as an intensive program for personal growth. The program and its environment establish the possibility to explore the higher dimensions of life and offers tools to re-engineer one's self through the inner science of yoga. Once given the tools to rejuvenate, people can optimize all aspects of health, inner growth and success. For those seeking professional and personal excellence, this program offers keys for meaningful and fulfilling relationships at work, home, community, and most importantly, within one's self.

Inner Engineering can be thought of as a synthesis of holistic sciences to help participants establish an inner foundation and vision for all dimensions of life and find the necessary balance between the challenges of a hectic career and the inner longing for peace and wellbeing.

The approach is a modern antidote to stress, and presents simple but powerful processes from yogic science to purify the system and increase health and inner wellbeing. Program components include guided meditations and transmission of the sacred Shambhavi Mahamudra. When practiced on a regular basis, these tools have the potential to enhance one's experience of life on many levels.

# Isha Yoga Center

Isha Yoga Center, founded under the aegis of Isha Foundation, is located on 150 acres of lush land at the foothills of the Velliangiri Mountains that are part of the Nilgiris Biosphere, a reserve forest with abundant wildlife.

Created as a powerful *sthana* (a center for inner growth), this popular destination attracts people from all parts of the world. It is unique in its offering of all aspects of yoga – *gnana* (knowledge), *karma* (action), *kriya* (energy), and *bhakti* (devotion) and revives the *Guru-shishya parampara* (the traditional method of knowledge transfer from master to disciple).

Isha Yoga Center provides a supportive environment for people to shift to healthier lifestyles, improve interpersonal relationships, seek a higher level of self-fulfilment, and realize their full potential.

The Center is located 30 km west of Coimbatore, a major industrial city in South India which is well connected by air, rail, and road. All major national airlines operate regular flights into Coimbatore from Chennai, Delhi, Mumbai, and Bangalore. Train services are available from all major cities in India. Regular bus and taxi services are also available from Coimbatore to the Center.

Visitors are advised to contact the Center for availability and reservation of accommodation well in advance, as it is generally heavily booked.

# Dhyanalinga Yogic Temple

The Dhyanalinga is a powerful and unique energy form created by Sadhguru from the essence of yogic sciences. Situated at the Isha Yoga Center, the Dhyanalinga is the first of its kind to be completed in over 2000 years. The Dhyanalinga Yogic Temple is a meditative space that does not ascribe to any particular faith or belief system nor does it require any ritual, prayer, or worship.

The Dhyanalinga was consecrated by Sadhguru after three years of an intense process of *prana pratishtha*. Housed within an architecturally striking pillarless dome structure, the Dhyanalinga's energies allow even those unaware of meditation to experience a deep state of meditativeness, revealing the essential nature of life.

A special feature of the temple complex are the Theerthakunds, consecrated subterranean water bodies, energized by *rasalingas*. A dip in these vibrant pools significantly enhances one's spiritual receptivity and is a good preparation to receive the Grace of the Dhyanalinga. The waters of the Theerthakunds also rejuvenate the body, and bring health and wellbeing.

The Dhyanalinga Yogic Temple draws many thousands of people every week, who converge to experience a deep sense of inner peace.

*Body: The Greatest Gadget*

# *Worldwide Centers*

INDIA

Isha Yoga Center, Velliangiri Foothills, Semmedu (P.O.), Coimbatore 641114 India.

Telephone: +91-422-2515345

Email: info@ishafoundation.org

USA

Isha Institute of Inner Sciences, 951 Isha Lane, McMinnville, TN 37110 USA.

Telephone: +1-931-668-1900

Email: usa@ishafoundation.org

UK

Isha Foundation, PO Box 559, Isleworth TW7 5WR, UK.

Telephone: +44-79 56 99 87 29

Email: uk@ishafoundation.org

AUSTRALIA

Isha Foundation Australia, Suite 1.5, 173 Lennox Street, Richmond VIC 3121, Melbourne, Australia.

Telephone: +61 433 643 215

Email: australia@ishafoundation.org

SINGAPORE

Isha Singapore, Block 805, 05-636, Chai Chee Road, Singapore 460805.

Telephone: +65 96660197

Email: singapore@ishafoundation.org

MALAYSIA

Telephone: +60 17-366-5252

Email: malaysia@ishafoundation.org

MIDDLE EAST

Telephone: 961-3-789-046, 961-3-747-178

Email: lebanon@ishafoundation.org